KIDS
IN THE GARDEN

Growing Plants for Food and Fun

BY Elizabeth McCorquodale

black dog publishing
london uk

CONTENTS

76 RECIPES

INTRODUCTION

There is something very special about growing plants. It's a little bit like magic, and that makes you, the gardener, the magician. Take one little seed, add some soil, water, warmth and sunlight and it changes into a plant. The hard seed coating splits open and from that tiny case, leaves and stem shoot up and grow. A flower unfolds and a fruit swells and ripens. Now that is real magic.

To grow up healthy and happy all plants need the right sort of soil and the right amount of sun, warmth and water. The trick of being a good gardener is to give your plants what they want most. Look at the symbols in the "know it all" section at the bottom of each project page to help you give your plants the best conditions.

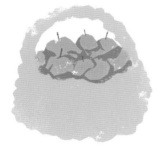

SOWING TO
HARVEST TIME

HOW MUCH SUN

HOW MUCH
WATER

COMPANION
PLANTS

PESTS

DISTANCE BETWEEN
PLANTS

GERMINATION
TIME

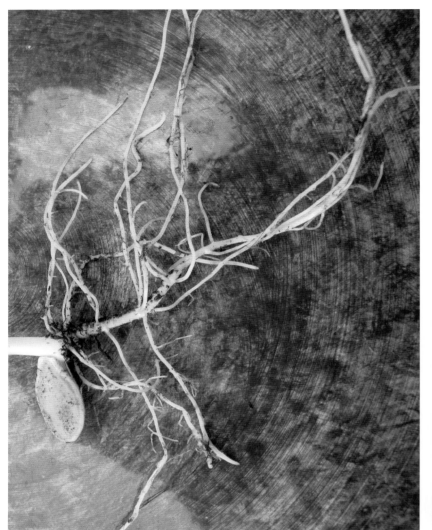

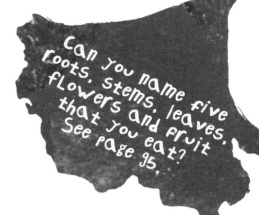

Can you name five roots, stems, leaves, flowers and fruit that you eat? See page 95.

PARTS OF A PLANT

Each part of a plant has a special job to do in the same way as each part of you has a special job. You have legs to walk with and eyes to see with and a heart to pump your blood around your body. Plants aren't as complicated as human beings, but they still manage to do some rather clever things.

Roots anchor the plant in the ground. The fine, hairy roots suck up the lovely watery 'soup' from the soil which is the plants' everyday food. The thicker roots store some food for the plant to use later.

The **stem** or trunk of a plant is there to hold the leaves up towards the light and to pump the food nutrients all around the plant. Inside all stems are a collection of tubes, like drinking straws, that carry the watery soup from the soil up through the stems and to the leaves. These can be easily seen in a celery stick.

The **leaves** are food factories for the plant. The leaves contain a green chemical called "chlorophyll" which together with the light from the sun make sugars for the plant to use as food. They also make oxygen for us to breathe.

Flowers are there to make seeds which will grow into new plants. Flowers are often colorful and sweet-smelling so that they attract birds and insects that will help them to make new plants. They also make a sugary syrup called "nectar" and nutritious pollen which reward the creatures who visit them.

Most of us think of **fruit** as sweet and tasty food to eat, but according to scientists a fruit is the part of the plant that contains seeds. Some fruit, like peas and tomatoes, aren't sweet at all and we think of them as vegetables. And some foods, like figs, that we think of as fruit, are really flowers!

PHOTOSYNTHESIS

Plant leaves are food and oxygen factories. They make sugars for themselves and oxygen for the world.

Plants re-cycle our old air and turn it into clean fresh air for us to use again. Energy from the sun is stored by the plant in the green chemical called chlorophyll in its leaves. The plant uses this energy, like a thousand mini-battery packs, to power a process called "photosynthesis". This is when water and carbon dioxide gas combine in the leaves to make sugars (for the plant) and oxygen (for us).

Sunlight + carbon dioxide
+ water + chlorophyll
= food for plant + oxygen for us

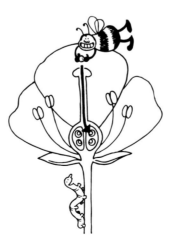

POLLINATION AND FERTILIZATION

Seeds are made when two part of a flower —the male pollen and the female ovules— are brought together. The pollen, which is like orange or yellow grains of icing sugar, is made on the male anthers of a flower. When the pollen is dusted onto the stigma, either by the wind or with the help of a bird or insect, the pollen sticks to the top of the stigma. That is pollination.

From there the pollen sends a tube down the female style where it lands on the ovules. The pollen joins with the ovule and together they make a seed. This is called "fertilization". Snug and secure within the ovary, the seed grows and matures.

THE CARBON CYCLE

All animals, including humans, have a rather good arrangement with our friends in the plant world. Plants exhale oxygen and we animals inhale it and use it to live on. And in turn we exhale carbon dioxide and the plants use that to live on. It works so well, and keeps our earth so healthy that our world has worked like this for millions and millions of years. The trouble is our pollution is creating too much carbon dioxide and the cycle isn't working properly anymore.

GERMINATION

Germination happens when a seed splits open and begins life as a plant. Each seed, even the tiniest, contains roots, shoots and leaves, all waiting to burst out and begin to grow. To do this the seed must be given the right amount of water, warmth and light. Seeds are tough and can live, protected by the outer shell, for a long, long time. Different types of seeds need different conditions to trigger them to grow. Plants that grow in cold climates may not be able to germinate unless the seed is given a cold spell, in a fridge perhaps, to trick them into believing they have lived through the Winter. Desert seeds may only need a light shower of rain to trigger them to sprout.

SEED DISPERSAL

If all the seeds from a plant fell and germinated right beside the parent plant there wouldn't be enough light and soil for all the seeds to grow. Nature has invented many different ways to scattering seeds around the world. Some methods scatter them only a short distance away from the parent plant, like the exploding capsules of busy lizzie plants. Others are designed to send their seeds thousands of miles away, like the floating seeds of coconut palms.

How are these seeds dispersed? Sweet fruits and tasty seeds? Fluffy, light seeds? Exploding capsules? Spiny and sticky seeds? See page 95.

How old are the oldest living seeds ever found? See page 95.

GROWING HEALTHY PLANTS

Plants need five things to grow and stay healthy and happy. They need somewhere to live, food, air, water and warmth.

LIGHT

Seedlings like a bright spot out of direct sun. They can be delicate, and they'll dry out if it's too hot and they will grow thin and leggy in the shade as they stretch towards the light.

Some mature plants like it shady and others like to sunbathe, but most fruit and vegetables will tolerate a wide range of light levels.

Put your plants in a spot out of direct sun for a few days when you move them outside for the first time. Even plants get sunburn!

GARDEN SOIL

The best soils for growing fruit and veggies in your garden is one that doesn't dry out too quickly or stay soggy for too long. All soils will be better with lots of compost and well rotted organic manure mixed in. Young plants need a fine, crumbly texture to make it easier to send their delicate roots deep into the ground.

SOIL FOR POTS AND BASKETS

If you have to buy soil mix from the shop, look out for one that has a label saying it is organic and peat free which won't contain nasty chemicals. Peat is a type of earth that has taken hundreds and hundreds of years to make and if we use it, it will be gone forever!

You can make up your own potting soil by using some of your own garden soil mixed with kitchen compost (see page 15).

PLANT FOODS AND FERTILIZERS

Plants make some of their own food themselves. They get the rest of what they need from the nutrient-rich liquid in the soil. The different kinds of nutrients that plants need all have special scientific names. The three main foods are Nitrogen for healthy leaves and strong growth, Phosphate for strong roots and Potassium (potash) for flowers and fruit.

NETTLE SOUP FOR PLANTS

You can make some nutritious and delicious plant food (delicious for your plants, not you!) by soaking ordinary stinging nettles in water. Use rubber gloves to collect the nettles and put them in a large container, then cover them with water and a tight fitting lid. After a couple of weeks the 'soup' will be ready to use… the darker and smellier it is, the richer and more nutritious it is. Make it up by mixing one part nettle soup to 9 parts water. Water it onto your soil, not onto the leaves of your plants.

Other potash-rich plants that you can use and make up in exactly the same way are comfrey and horseradish leaves.

Tip... just before your mum invites the neighbors 'round is not the time to water your garden with nettle soup!

OTHER HOME-GROWN FERTILIZERS YOU CAN USE ARE:

• **Your hair!** next time you have a hair cut save your trimmings to use in your veggie plot… old fashioned gardeners always planted their hair along with their tomatoes.

• **Crushed egg shells** scattered in a ring around your plants will add lime and calcium to the soil and will deter slugs, who don't like the sharp edges.

• **Tea leaves and coffee grounds** are very good for adding to plants like blueberries and potatoes that like acid soil.

• **Well-rotted hamster, chicken, or horse manure** or the manure of any vegetarian pet is a great plant food. Mix it with your garden soil or use it to mulch the ground around your plants.

• **Wood ash** is very high in potash and is very good for spreading on the soil around your plants.

• **Comfrey** has long roots that collect nutrients from deep down in the soil. When you compost comfrey, or make a lovely stinky plant food from its leaves, it will return all those stored nutrients to your soil and plants.

• **Green manures** are plants which help to feed the soil and sometimes help to break it up, making it easier to dig. You can buy seeds of alfalfa, mustard, beans and clover to grow on your patch, and then dig them back in before you sow your Spring seeds.

• Some plants are terrific at capturing the goodness from the soil and from the air. Plants that belong to the **bean family** all have the knack of trapping nitrogen from the air and storing it in their roots. In Fall (Autumn), throw the plant tops onto the compost heap and dig the roots back into the soil so the trapped nitrogen can be used by your next crop.

WATERING AND THE WATER CYCLE

Plants need water to carry nutrients around inside them and to keep their cells firm and healthy. Cells are the tiny building blocks that all living things are made of.

There is a certain amount of water in our world—no more is ever added and none is ever taken away. Some is deep below us in underground lakes and rivers, some is in the streams, lakes and oceans, some is frozen in the North and South poles and some is floating above us in the clouds, waiting to fall on us as rain or snow.

We need very clean water to drink and to wash ourselves, so our tap water needs to be cleaned with chemicals and filters. And so that we don't send dirty water back into the water cycle, it needs to be cleaned again after it leaves us.

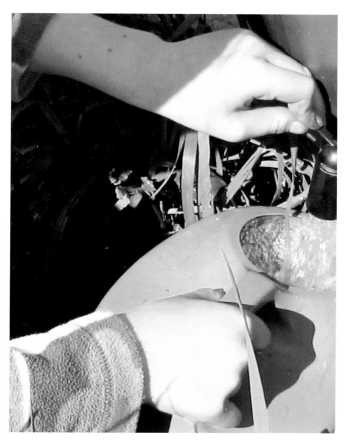

WATER IN THE GARDEN

Our gardens, though, don't need freshly cleaned water. They are quite happy with the water we have used in our baths, washing machines and sinks. As long as we use eco-friendly soaps we can use our waste water on our plants and gardens. Simple.

When you are growing fruit and veggies in containers the biggest problem is making sure your plants get the right amount of water—you can do this in three easy, eco-friendly ways.

1
Use the right type of soil—lots of well rotted compost with some added water-saving crystals or organic seaweed gel will hold the water in the soil ready for when your plants need it.

2
Make sure water can't evaporate easily by lining the sides of your containers with old plastic bags and mulching the top of the soil.

3
Put in a watering system… a saucer under your pot and an upturned bottle with tiny holes punched into the lid pushed into the compost will cut down on the water which runs away, unused.

HOMEMADE COMPOST

Compost is the stuff you get when you combine the right waste and rubbish from around your home, give it a bit of a stir and leave it for a while. In goes all the stuff you don't want from your garden and all the fruit and veggie scraps from your kitchen, and out comes lovely nutritious soil for you to grow more stuff in your garden. Wow, what a perfect cycle! Sounds easy, doesn't it? That's because it is. But... compost doesn't make itself. It needs you!

Compost, like a plant, needs warmth, sun, air and moisture. Too much of one thing will make it sit and sulk.

In the Summer it can take only eight weeks to make a whole pile of rich, dark soil out of the stuff you would normally throw away!

HOW TO BUILD YOUR COMPOST HEAP

Build it in a sunny spot and start with a six inch layer of browns. Cover with a six inch layer of greens, then a six inch layer of browns. Keep on going... greens, browns, greens, browns.... Every now and then add a shovel-full of soil from your garden... this will contain many of the mini-beasts and micro organisms that help to make a healthy heap. Water occasionally when your heap gets dry (dry waste doesn't rot). Keep your heap covered with a large piece of old carpet, cardboard or plastic to keep the heat in, and the weather out. Turn your heap over or stir it around as often as you can and at least every three or four weeks for the quickest compost.

• Greens
Fruit and vegetable peelings, hamster, rabbit and bird bedding, grass clippings and weeds, tea bags, coffee grounds, egg shells, nettles, comfrey and pea and bean roots.

• Browns
Newspapers, scrunched up into balls, cardboard (shredded and torn), Fall (Autumn) leaves.

• Not Wanted
Cooked food, cat or dog waste or the litter from any meat-eating pet, any meat or fat.

MULCH

A mulch is something that you put on top of your soil. There are all sorts of mulches and they do all sorts of jobs.

- Mulching saves water by slowing down evaporation.
- Mulching saves work by stopping weeds from growing.
- Mulching can stop beasties from attacking your plants.
- Mulching can help to warm up the soil in the Spring to give your plants a head-start.

TYPES OF MULCHES

- Gravel • Old carpets • Straw
- Compost • Bark/wood chippings
- Old pet bedding (from rabbits or chickens) • Plastic • Grass cuttings
- Green manures • Newspaper
- Cardboard

BE A WORM FARMER

Making a wormery is another way of turning waste into soil and food for your plants. Worms eat leaves and kitchen scraps and turn them into a rich, crumbly soil that is perfect for growing hungry plants like tomatoes and peppers. And they also produce a strong liquid plant food for watering onto your garden.

1
Choose a spot for your wormery that will not get too cold or too hot. In the Winter a wormery will do very well in a garage or frost-free shed. Drill a hole for the cork or tap 1" (2 cm) up from the base of the bin. Make sure that the hole is small enough to make a very tight seal around the tap or cork.

2
Drill a ring of air holes about 3½" (9 cm) apart just under the rim of the lid.

3
Fill the bottom of your bin with 4" (10 cm) of gravel or coarse sand.

4
Cut the plastic sheet so it fits neatly over the layer of gravel, with no gaps around the edges. Poke plenty of drainage holes through the plastic to allow the worm juice to drain through and collect in the gravel beneath.

5
Put an 3" (8 cm) layer of compost or leaf-mould/garden soil mix on top of the plastic. Put your worms on this.

6
Place a litre or so of vegetable or fruit scraps on the compost and cover it with several layers of wet (but not dripping) newspaper. Replace the lid and leave your worms to make themselves at home for a couple of weeks. From then on keep adding kitchen scraps whenever the last scraps have been used up. Don't over-feed or under-feed your worms and don't let them get too wet or too dry.

Wormery Worries.... Stinky wormery and dead worms means too much moisture or too much food.

Use your worm juice by diluting one part juice to ten parts water.

You will need:

- A plastic bin, such as a medium-sized garbage bin or a deep box with a lid

- A sturdy cork or a rain barrel (water-butt) tap

- A piece of thick polythene (plastic) sheet

- A small bag of gravel or very coarse sand

- Compost from a compost heap, or well rotted leaf-mould mixed with garden soil

- At least 200 tiger or brandling worms (these can be captured from a mature compost heap or ordered from a wormery supplier)

SAVING SEEDS

Saving seeds from your own plants is easy! You may even have enough seeds to start a seed swap with other gardening friends.

Collect **small seeds** by cutting the whole seed head after the flowers have faded and before the little seeds have fallen to the ground. Pop the seed head in a paper bag and hang it upside down somewhere very dry. When they are ripe, the seeds will drop out of the seed head and into the bottom of your paper bag. Once all the seeds have dropped, remove the empty seed head, seal the bag and label it.

Larger seeds, like **nasturtiums**, can be picked up where they drop from the plant, left to dry on a piece of newspaper and then put in a labelled envelope.

Peas and beans can be left to dry on the plant if the weather is dry, or the whole plant can be pulled up and hung up in a warm and airy spot. Once they are dry and the pods are crisp, remove the shells and store the seeds in an envelope, or if you have lots to store, in a jar with a tight lid.

Wait until **tomatoes and cucumbers and squash** begin to get very soft, then open them up, collect the seeds and leave them to dry. When the seeds are completely dry, gently scrape them up, bag and label them.

Protect your seeds from moisture and high temperatures by tucking the bags into an air-tight container like a sandwich box and leave them in a cool, dark, dry place until you are ready to use them.

If you let a plant go to seed, it will think its job is done and it will stop making any flowers and fruit. Wait until late in the season before you let your plants develop seeds

BASIC TOOLS AND EQUIPMENT

Gardeners need tools. Something to dig with, to cut with, something to turn the soil and to protect our hands.

• Choose **gloves** that aren't too tight. Rubber washing up gloves are great for collecting stinging nettles, but any gloves will help to keep your hands clean.
• **Spades** are used to cut chunks out of the soil and to dig holes for planting large plants like fruit bushes.
• **Garden forks** are great for breaking up the soil and turning it over.
• **Hand forks** and trowels are needed to dig small holes and for gardening in pots.
• **Hoes** are one of a gardener's best friends! Using a hoe is the quickest and easiest way of weeding your veggie patch. The sharp edge slices the top off the weeds so you can collect them to put on the compost heap.
• A **garden rake** is great for levelling the surface of the soil after digging, and for collecting up weeds after you have hoed.
• **String**—you need something to tie your tall plants onto their supports.
• **Canes** are usually made from bamboo and are very strong. If you know someone who grows **bamboo** in their garden, you may be able to harvest some to use as climbing supports for your tall plants.
• **Pea sticks** are thin, twiggy sticks cut from bushes that gardeners use to support pea plants. Peas like to grow up these better than canes because they let the pea plants spread out.
• **Scissors** are the best tool for snipping herbs like chives and cress and for cutting string to tie up your cucumbers and tomatoes.
• **Secateurs** are for serious gardeners, but they must be used with great care. They are needed to cut tough plants and branches.

LABELS, LABELS, LABELS

When you are gardening you need to remember what you have planted and when you planted it… it's so easy to forget, especially if you are growing lots of seedlings.

HERE ARE SOME IDEAS FOR LABELS

• Smooth stones and waterproof paint or indelible markers • Sticky labels for indoor pots • Popsicle sticks • Clothes pegs clipped to the side of the pot • Milk bottle labels

For labelling trays of seedlings, cut lots of strips from an old milk bottle and write on each one with a permanent marker. Plants in the garden need something bigger and sturdier. Search out some strong, straight sticks and a couple of plastic milk bottles. Cut some chunky rectangles from the plastic bottles, cut two slits down one edge and thread the flag onto the stick Write the name of the plant, and the date of planting onto your flag.

Wooden markers—bits of scrap wood make very good labels for large pots and in your garden patch. Cut one end of the wood into an arrow shape to make it easier to push down into the soil.

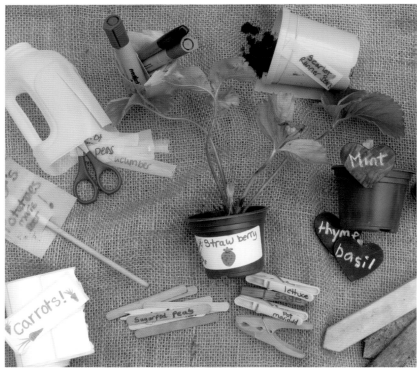

PLANNING YOUR GARDEN

GARDENING IN POTS

Plants in pots need feeding regularly... try making your own plant food (page 11) or buy organic fertilizer and water it in.

All the plants in this book can be grown in pots. The nifty thing is to make your pots fun to look at and easy to look after. Always add water crystals or seaweed granules to the soil in your pots to cut down on watering and always cover the bare soil with mulch to stop evaporation.

You can use almost anything as a container as long as you can put drainage holes in the bottom to let water drain away—baskets, bags, old prams, yogurt pots, old tyres, holey wheelbarrows, tea cups and coffee pots, tin cans, egg boxes, boots, baths and, of course—plant pots. You can even make your own out of old comics or newspapers!

Choose large containers for thirsty plants like zucchini (courgettes) so they won't dry out quickly, and for tall plants like fruit trees, to stop them being blown over. Look around. What can you see? What can you use?

If your garden is a balcony or a patio you can still grow lots of fruit, veggies and tasty herbs. You can even grow fruit trees. Protect your plants from the wind with dense garden netting and tie tall plants securely to stop them blowing over.

BEDS AND BORDERS

Growing your food plants in the soil in your garden or allotment is great fun. To make it as easy as possible just follow these four simple steps.

1 Find a sunny spot away from the roots of trees.

2 Dig out all the weeds you see and get rid of all the roots and any seeds that you find.

3 Add as much compost or well rotted manure as you can. This helps the texture (how crumbly the soil is) and the nutrients (how much plant food it holds).

4 Dig your garden… and dig and dig! Your new plants—and seeds especially—will grow faster, bigger and better if their roots have a lovely crumbly soil to grow down into. Imagine the difference between trying to push delicate roots down through hard, stony soil or through soft crumbly soil— which would you prefer?

Draw out your garden plot. Measure how big it is and decide what you want to grow. Don't forget to add in bee plants and companion plants to keep your garden healthy!

It is easier to spot weed invaders if you sow your seeds in straight rows.

Always remember to leave enough space to walk between your plants without stepping on them. See the "know it all" strip to see how much room to leave between rows.

Bigger plots, especially those that are planted with very large amounts of one type of vegetable, are often planted "in rotation". This means that each year, each type of plant is grown in a different place. This is done because some pests and diseases stay in the soil, so if the same plant was to be grown in the same place year after year the pests would be there, ready and waiting to attack them each time.

Square foot gardening is a garden space where every little bit of room is used all the time. It isn't really only one square foot, but it is only about one square yard (metre), which is then divided up into smaller sections. The trick is to keep on planting… if you plant something that is quite slow to begin with, like zucchini (courgettes), you can plant something beside it that will grow very quickly, like radishes. As soon as you pull up a lettuce you plant another one. This is a fun way to garden, and great if you don't have much space.

CLIMBING TRELLIS 6' TALL

TALL SUGARSNAP PEAS ×48			
CUT + COME AGAIN LETTUCE			
SALAD ONIONS ×144	CARROTS ×36	CARROTS ×36	CHIVES ×4
CALENDULA ×9	BUSH BEANS ×9	BUSH BEANS ×9	NASTURTIUMS ×4
COURGETTE ×1 +RADISHES	BEETS ×36	BEETS ×36	PUMPKIN ×1 +RADISHES

4'

PLAN FOR A SQUARE FOOT GARDEN

GARDENING ON THE WILD SIDE

A community of plants, birds, animals and insects—and you!

Your garden is part of something called an "ecosystem". This means that it works with the sun, the air, the rain and the soil and with all the creatures, big and small, to make a good and healthy world.

Super tidy gardens, with no beasties at all and lots of clean bare soil are not super healthy gardens.

A healthy garden has a good mix of plants and beasties that all work together to make a beautiful and productive plot.

A small pile of logs, a compost heap corralled by a twiggy fence, an old pile of leaves; all these will attract beetles, slugs and centipedes that will help to build a fantastic mini-world. Leave a little pile of twigs or small branches in a cosy corner… these make an ideal hiding place for small mammals, reptiles and amphibians. These little animals will help to clean up weed seeds and pests.

Amphibians… amphibians are animals that live part of their lives in water and part on land. Can you name five? See page 95.

Small mammals… mammals give birth to live young and feed their babies on milk. Can you name five small mammals that you could find in a garden? See page 95.

Reptiles… reptiles are cold blooded animals with back bones. They have scaly skin. Can you name five reptiles that you could find in a garden? See page 95.

LOGPILE HIGH-RISE

A pile of logs in the corner of the garden can do many things. First it provides a snug home for beetles and other creatures who thrive in the dark woody dampness of rotting logs and damp earth. Secondly, small mammals and amphibians visit the log pile to hunt the creatures who live there.

Without fungi and the beetle grubs, woodlice and all the other fascinating creatures who eat rotting wood we would all be living in a woodpile! As trees fall down there would be nothing to chew up the wood and break it down into the humus that makes the soil.

BIRDS

Birds are beautiful and fascinating and they do a terrific job of tidying up the mini-beasts and weed seeds in your garden. You can encourage them in by giving them somewhere to perch and something extra to eat. Many birds eat both seeds and insects, especially in the Spring when they are feeding their chicks.

HOW TO MAKE A BIRD FEEDER

Encourage birds onto your patch by giving them tasty treats. You can make a bird feeder out of a plastic bottle and fill it with good quality bird seed.

1
Choose a plastic drinks bottle and mark a dot on opposite sides of the bottle, about 4" (10 cm) up from the bottom. To make the perch, press a thumb tack (drawing pin) into the dots to start your hole. Use the scissors to enlarge these holes and push the stick through so it pokes out evenly each side.

2
Mark two more dots 2" (5 cm) above the perch. Press the thumb tack in to start the holes and enlarge them with the scissors. These are the seed holes so they must be big enough to allow the birds to peck at the seed.

3
Just below the cap, make two small holes and push the garden wire through. Twist it to make a loop so you can hang your feeder over a branch.

4
Push holes into the bottom of the bottle to let any water that collects inside the bottle drain away.

5
Fill your feeder with good quality bird seed and adjust the feeding holes so that the seed can be poked out but doesn't fall out by itself. Hang up your feeder and keep watch!

Beware! New seedlings are a great treat for pigeons, and plump flower buds attract bullfinches who can strip a fruit tree of new buds before you know it. Of course, all those delicious berries are just as yummy for other creatures as they are for you, so cover them up. Strings of old CDs catch and reflect the light and can scare some birds away. Garden netting or old net curtains draped over your fruit bushes will stop birds from pinching the good stuff and allow them to tidy up the bad guys instead. After you have picked all the fruit, don't forget to take the netting away and move the CDs to another plant so the birds can move back in and feast on any pests that have colonized your fruit trees and bushes.

You will need:

- A plastic drinks bottle and lid
- Bird seed
- Garden wire
- Thin sticks
- Scissors
- Drawing pin (thumb tack)
- Marker pen

Hang your bird feeder up well away from cat hidey holes so nothing can creep up on your birds on silent paws!

Bumble bees shake the pollen loose by vibrating their wing muscles at over 200 beats per second.

This is a Bee Bank
Please look after my bees

BEE RESCUE

Honey bees and bumble bees visit our plants in search of nectar, a sugary syrup, and pollen, the yellow or orange powder that is made on the male part of flowers. In return for this treat the bees pollinate the flowers, dusting pollen grains from one flower onto another so the flowers can begin to make seeds.

But bumble bees are special… and some plants can be pollinated only by bumble bees. When a bumble bee visits the flower it grabs the anther and gives it a good shake. Like someone emptying a salt cellar, this shakes the pollen out of the tiny holes in the anther. This is called "buzz pollination". Other insects can visit these plants but they won't be able to pollinate them, because they don't buzz pollinate. If they're not pollinated, the flowers can't make seed or fruit… or new plants.

Bees are able to pick up pollen so easily because the hair on their bodies holds a static charge of electricity that attracts the pollen grains… the same as the static that you make when you rub a balloon over your hair.

Some bees carry the pollen around in 'baskets' on their legs. They use their front legs to brush the pollen off their hair and collect it in their pollen baskets.

All bumble bees sit on their eggs, like chickens, to hatch them. And like chickens, they have a little bare patch on their fronts so that the warmth from their bodies can warm their eggs. The mother bee makes a tiny pot of honey from the nectar she collects from the flowers in your garden and keeps it beside her to sip from as she sits in her nest… to keep this filled up she needs to visit hundreds of flowers each day. You can help by planting lots of bee plants in your garden, especially those that flower in the Spring.

A TEA-POT, A BEE-POT!

Different kinds of bumble bees need different kinds of nests. One type chooses old mouse nests that have narrow entrance tunnels and are already full of nesting material. You can give them the same comfy home right in your garden by filling an old tea pot with natural nesting material and burying it in a sheltered spot.

1 Make sure the tea pot is clean and dry. Put a layer of pebbles in the bottom to keep the bedding off the base of the pot.

2 Fill the tea pot loosely with the bedding. It can be all one kind or a mixture of whatever you are able to find. Leave space in the pot for the air and your bee to move around.

3 Dig a hole in a spot in your garden just big enough to hold your bee pot. Bury your pot, but leave the spout and the lid uncovered… your bee will use the spout as a doorway and if you are very careful you can use the lid to peak inside the bee pot in the early Spring to check on them.

4 Prop the flat stone over the bee pot to deflect the rain. Now sit back and wait for your bumble to find your pot.

You will need:

- An old tea pot with a lid (check inside to make sure there is no strainer at the bottom of the spout)
- Lots of soft, dry, natural materials, like dry moss, tufts of animal fur, delicate leaves
- A few pebbles
- A large flat stone or a tile

OTHER THINGS YOU CAN DO TO BE BEE FRIENDLY

Make a mud brick and leave it in a sunny spot. Lots of insects will visit it and fly away with little lumps of dry mud to build their nests.

Roughly dig over a patch of ground in a warm and sunny spot. Put a twiggy little fence around it and post a sign. "Keep out. Bees Nesting". Solitary bees will make little tunnels in the soil, in which to hatch their eggs.

Plant lots of bee plants in your garden alongside your fruit and vegetables. If you plant at least five of these plants, you will be making a great start: mint, lavender, sage, rosemary, chives, marjoram, comfrey, sunflowers, or cornflowers.

BEE LODGE

Make a Bee Lodge out of a clay pot. Cut some hollow lengths of bamboo to fit snugly inside the pot and hold them in place with tape and modelling clay. Place your bee box on a sunny, dry spot in the garden where it won't be disturbed. Tip it slightly downwards so that rain can't get in, and wedge it in place with stones. It won't be too long until you have your first lodgers!

PEST PATROL

With your wildlife-friendly garden you will have plenty of creatures who are on your side in the battle against garden pests. But at certain times you may need some extra help, such as when you have lots of tiny seedlings or if you are growing a plant that some beastie finds irresistible. Lots of pests can be kept away from your crops by placing a barrier in their way.

Pigeons can be stopped from pulling up tasty new seedlings by laying netting over the soil.

Butterflies and carrot fly can be prevented from laying eggs on your plants by using a finer net, snugly pegged down around the edges. Beetle grubs and cutworms can be kept away by fitting a

little planting ring over each plant, made from cardboard tubes or plastic bottles.

The easiest **slug traps** are simply planks of wood or squares of heavy cardboard placed directly onto damp soil—slugs love the damp, dark conditions and you can just pick them up and dispose of your unwanted guests! If you are squeamish you can pick them up with gloves or make a slug scooper out of a plastic bottle.

A **slug cafe** is made by sinking several shallow bowls into your garden close to the plants that your slugs like most. Fill them with beer or milk and put a tile, over the top to make it damp, dark and inviting. Empty your traps every few days and refill with fresh bait.

Do you know that not all slugs are a gardeners' enemy? Many slugs feed on rotting vegetation like fallen leaves and old fruit, and others are carnivores who eat garden pests like other slugs, beetle grubs and snails.

Aphids, greenfly and blackfly
swarm over the tender, young growing tips of plants and there can be so many of them that they can stop a plant growing properly. They also make a sugary liquid called "honeydew" that ants love. Like farmers, the ants protect their flock of aphids from predators so they can have the honeydew. And if that wasn't bad enough there is a horrid black mould that grows on honeydew which can get so thick that the plant will die. Luckily ladybirds, hoverfly larva and lacewings all feast on aphids, and if your garden is already a good place to be for these helpful insects, aphids should never get out of control.

Pick–a–pest Caterpillars, slugs, snails and aphid groups can all be picked off easily and disposed of.

Encourage hoverflies to come into your patch by planting lots of nectar rich plants right alongside your beans and broad beans and giving them somewhere to nest.

Are you any good with chopsticks? How about slug-sticks?

Dot your herbs and flowers around the garden to attract a variety of insects and birds into your garden.

COME IN

LADYBIRD AND LACEWING LODGE

Ladybirds and lacewings need somewhere warm and dry to hibernate over the Winter You can help by making a ladybird lodge out of a large drinks bottle, some twigs and some cardboard.

1 Cut the bottle just below the shoulder of the bottle, to make a tube with one open end.

2 Cut the cardboard across the bumps to make a length 2" (5 cm) shorter than the length of your bottle. The cardboard will get soggy if it sticks out at all. Roll up the cardboard and fit it into the bottle.

3 Push twigs into the gaps in the cardboard. Let some of the twigs stick out a bit so that the ladybirds and lacewings have somewhere to land.

4 Push the lodge securely, with the opening pointing slightly downwards, into an evergreen hedge or a dense shrub and leave it undisturbed.

You will need:

- A large plastic drinks bottle with the top cut away
- A piece of corrugated cardboard
- A selection of thin twigs (hollow ones are great)
- Heavy-duty scissors

COMPANION PLANTS... YOUR FRIENDS IN THE GARDEN

Plants help each other in many different ways.

Some **disguise** the scent of your fruit and veggies so that the insect that would normally feed on them can't sniff them out. Carrot root fly searches out your carrots by smell—onions, chives and other very scented plants confuse the carrot fly so it can't find them

Trap crops are plants that insects love to feed on, so they will choose to eat the trap crop instead of your veggies. Cabbage—white caterpillars love cabbages but they also love nasturtiums, so plant them close by to keep your veggies safe.

Repellant crops have a strong smell that some insects don't like. Would you go near a place that stank? Geraniums have an odour that flies and mosquitoes can't stand.

Some plants produce a **chemical** from their roots that drives away or kills harmful bugs in the soil. Marigolds keep tiny harmful worms called "nematodes" away from tomatoes.

Grow a **good mix of plants** in your garden. Include fruit, veggies, herbs and flowers and make sure your plants are happy by giving them the conditions they like best.

HOW TO PLANT SEEDS

Small seeds need to be planted on or near the surface of the soil. They are very delicate and need just the right amount of warmth, water and light to grow into healthy plants. You can help them to do this by following these easy instructions.

1 Fill a small pot with soil almost to the top. Water your soil and let the water drain away.

2 Put a pinch of seed in one hand and using the thumb and forefinger of the other hand pick up the tiny seeds and sprinkle them carefully onto the soil. Leave enough room between the seeds to allow them space to grow. Gently press the seeds into the surface of the soil.

3 Give your seeds a careful watering using your seed sprinkler.

4 Write the name of the plant and the date onto your label with a waterproof pen and tuck the label into the pot.

5 Push two popsicle sticks down each side of the pot and slip a plastic bag over the top. This will stop water evaporating and stop the soil and your seeds drying out too quickly.

6 Place your planted pot in a warm, bright place. Make sure it doesn't get direct sunlight or your seeds will bake! Water your seeds when the soil begins to dry out. Once most of your tiny seedlings have appeared, remove their cover and move them to a sunny spot to grow into strong and healthy plants.

Larger seeds need to be planted deeper in the soil or they will topple over when they begin to grow. With a lolly stick, make a hole about 1" (3 cm) into your soil. You can do this easily by measuring 1" on a ruler and marking it onto your stick. Drop your seed into the hole, firm it in. and water it gently.

You will need:

- **Small pots with drainage holes to allow the water to drain away**
- **Soil**
- **Watering can or seed sprinkler**
- **Label and waterproof pen**
- **Small plastic bag**
- **Popsicle sticks**

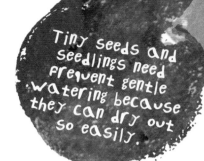

Tiny seeds and seedlings need frequent gentle watering because they can dry out so easily.

TAKING CUTTINGS

Some plants can be grown by cutting a twig and encouraging it to grow new roots. Not all plants can be grown this way, but many can, and very easily too. Take your cuttings in Spring or early Summer when plants are doing most of their growing. Many of the herbs and all bush fruit can be grown from cuttings.

1 Choose a plant pot and fill it to near the top with some sandy soil. The sand will increase drainage and help to stop the twig from rotting before it can make new roots.

2 Cut a twig from near the top of your chosen plant. Choose a healthy twig that is about 6" (18 cm) long and no thicker than a drinking straw. Make the cut just below a leaf joint (where a leaf grows from the twig). If your cutting is very leafy, trim some of the lower leaves off so the twig puts all its energy into making new roots instead of feeding old leaves.

3 With one of your popsicle sticks make a hole in the compost and push the cutting half way down into the soil and tuck it in firmly. Write your label, not forgetting the date, and slip it into the pot.

4 Water the soil well, and let the water drain away. Try not to get any water on the leaves.

5 Tuck the lolly sticks down the sides of the pot and place the plastic bag over the top. The lolly sticks should hold the bag away from the leaves so that they don't rot.

6 Place your pot in a warm, bright spot, but out of direct sunlight. Keep an eye on the soil and water it when it begins to dry out.

7 Wait until new roots grow—some plants, like mint, grow very quickly but others which have woodier stems take longer to root. Check for new roots every week by giving the stem a very gently tug. If new roots have grown the stem will hold tight to the soil... and you have a fine new plant.

You will need:

- **Scissors or secateurs**

- **A plant pot (make sure it has drainage holes)**

- **Soil with some sand mixed in**

- **Label and waterproof pen**

- **Popsicle sticks**

- **Small plastic bag**

- **Rooting hormone (some plants root better with the help of rooting powder, but many will root very well without it)**

LAYERING

Layering is a back-to-front way of taking cuttings… instead of cutting a stem and encouraging it to grow roots, you get it to grow the roots first and then cut the stem. Some plants, like strawberries, are so keen to grow in this way, that you hardly need to do anything at all! Rosemary, lemon balm, mint and raspberries can also be started from layering.

1 Choose a long flexible stem on your chosen plant and bend it over so that it touches the ground at a leaf joint.

2 Loosen the soil at the spot where the stem meets the ground so the new roots have a place to grow down into. Or you can bury a pot of soil in the ground so that it roots directly into the pot.

3 Peg the stem firmly in place so that the leaf joint is in snug contact with the soil.

4 Water it and leave it to root. This can take as little as two or three weeks with some plants in the Spring and Summer, or much longer in cooler months.

5 Check your plants every couple of weeks, and when you see a good clump of new roots growing, snip the stem that joins it to the parent plant. It is now ready to be moved to its new home… or maybe given to someone as a gift!

You will need:

• A plant

• A tent peg, some bent wire or even a heavy stone

• Some bare ground or a pot full of soil

DIVISION

Division is the quickest way of getting lots of new plants. If a clump-forming plant is getting too big, or you want lots of small plants instead of one big one, then all you need to do is dig up your plant, divide it up and replant it. Rhubarb, mint, marjoram, chives and comfrey can all be started from divisions.

1 Dig up your plant, making sure you dig up a good clump of roots.

2 Slice or pull the root clump into smaller pieces. Each piece must have a good set of roots from the bottom and stems or branches from the top. Long straggly roots can be snipped back tidily and the top of the plant can be given a bit of a haircut as well.

3 Replant your new plants into a fresh patch of garden or into pots. Make sure the soil is crumbly and loose to make the root run easy. Water very well and keep an eye on your new plants for a couple of weeks until they perk up and begin to grow again.

The roots have just had a bit of a bashing so they need tender loving care to help them recover and grow on strongly.

Give your new plants a good blanket of mulch to help them settle into their new home.

You will need:

- **A garden fork or spade**

- **New patch of ground or pots filled with soil**

- **Labels and a water-proof pen**

PROJECTS

SPROUTING SEEDS AND SHOOTS

Some of the fun of gardening is watching and waiting for a tiny seed to grow into a giant; but it's also great fun to sow some seeds that you will be able to harvest in just a few days or weeks.

You will need:

- **Seeds**
- **A wide-mouthed jar**
- **An elastic band**
- **A square of light fabric to fit over the top of the jar**

For a super speedy crop you can grow seed sprouts and shoots. Some are grown in jars and others in a pot, but either way you can be eating your first veggies in less than a week. Cress is one that we all know, but radishes, broccoli, beans and even sunflowers can be eaten when they are just mini-plants.

SHOOTS

Some seeds are so eager to germinate that they don't even need to be planted in order to grow… all they need is light, warmth, and water. We grow seed shoots so that we can enjoy the seeds and tiny new stems and we eat them before they've even had time to send out roots.

Sow your seeds in a damp, dark place and you will get long and leggy seedlings, delicious in stir-fries, sandwiches and salads. It's easy!

1
In a wide-mouthed jar sprinkle in a single layer of seeds and cover them with water. Cover the top of the jar with the fabric, held in place with an elastic band. Leave the seeds to soak in the water overnight.

2
In the morning, pour the water away and rinse the seeds several times with clean water. Drain again and leave your seeds in a spot away from direct light. In the evening rinse and drain your seeds again.

3
Continue to do this, morning and evening, until the seeds have germinated and long pale shoots have grown. Your shoots will be ready to eat when they are about 2" (5 cm) long.

4
You can keep your shoots fresh by storing them in a sealed container in the fridge for three or four days.

Remember to rinse your seed shoots every morning and evening to keep them fresh and tasty! Only ever use seeds that are recommended for growing as shoots or sprouts… not all seeds can be grown in this way!

Five of the best seeds for shoots: broccoli, radishes, chickpeas, peas and mung beans.

Five of the best seeds for sprouts: Mustard (this is a hot one!), cress, watercress, sunflowers, and alfalfa.

You will need:

- **Seeds**

- **A container (an egg shell, tea cup, recycled fruit punnet—what can you think of?)**

- **A very small amount of soil or you can use cotton wool, or paper towels instead.**

SPROUTS

Seed sprouts are different from shoots because they are grown in the light, and they are encouraged to grow roots.

1
Dampen the soil so it is moist but not too wet.

2
Sprinkle a thin layer of seeds onto the surface and press them down gently so that they are snuggled onto the surface.

3
Leave your seeds in a bright spot that doesn't get too hot. Water them when the soil dries out… this may be two or three times a day if it is very warm!

4
After only a few days your seeds will germinate and send up fresh green sprouts. Cut these when they are 2" (5 cm) tall and use them to perk up sandwiches and salads.

what do you get when two peas get in a fight?... Black eyed peas!

Watch out... the slugs are about. Slugs and snails adore bean shoots.

BEANS

Beans love deep, moist soil in full sun, so dig deep or give them a big pot to grow in. Climbing beans can shoot up a cane or pole up to 10' (3 metres) tall if you let them. Scarlet Runner Beans and other climbers like the yellow wax beans and purple Italian beans are perfect for training up canes into a wigwam.

You will need:

- **12 yoghurt pots (or similar) with drainage holes poked into the bottoms**
- **Soil**
- **Climbing bean seeds, all one type or a mixture of different kinds**
- **12 very tall canes or sturdy poles, at least 10' (3 metres) long**
- **Strong twine or string**
- **Kitchen compost and/or well rotted manure**
- **Plant food**

1 Plant two beans per pot by pushing them ½" into the soil. Label your pots and place them in a warm, bright spot like a sunny windowsill.

2 The seedlings will emerge from the soil in seven to ten days. Pinch out the weakest seedling and carefully push a short cane into the pot to give your bean something to climb up.

3 When the weather has grown warm and all danger of frost has passed, choose a sunny spot in your garden and push 12 canes very firmly 1' (30 cm) into the soil in the shape of a circle—but don't forget to leave room for a doorway! Tie all the canes together very tightly at the top to form a wigwam.

4 At the base of each cane, dig out a hole about 10" (25 cm) deep and 6" (15 cm) wide, then fill it back in with the excavated soil and plenty of kitchen compost.

5 Now tuck one bean plant into each hole, firm them in gently and loosely tie the tendrils to each cane. Water thoroughly. Mulch around your plants with sawdust or one of the other mulches listed on page 16.

6 Keep on watering your plants until they are scrambling up their poles. Keep an eye out for slugs and snails (see page 27) and remember to feed your plants regularly.

Beans love nettle soup! (see page 11)

When your plants begin to produce flowers it means that your first crop of beans isn't far away. Pick your beans when they are about 4 to 5" (10 to 13 cm) long for tasty whole beans, or leave them until they get a little longer to have as **string beans**. Older beans can be **shelled** and eaten in bean salads and bean pots. Remove the dried out pod and use the still-tender and tasty bean that is left. At the end of the season, when the weather is getting colder, the plants will begin to dry and wither. Harvest the last of the beans and put them somewhere cool to finish drying out. When they are completely **dry** you can store them in a glass jar to cook and eat in the Winter or save them to plant next Spring.

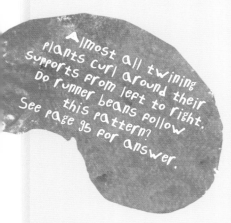
Almost all twining plants curl around their supports from left to right. Do runner beans follow this pattern? See page 95 for answer.

12 WEEKS

NASTURTIUMS

SNAILS SLUGS FLIES

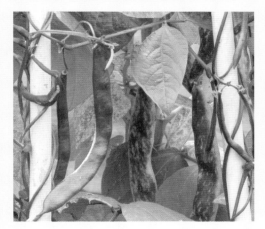

what is the fastest bean in the patch? a runner bean!

Garlicky Beans p76

Beany Burgers p76

Chilli Bean Wraps p76

PLANTS = 6"
ROWS = 24"

7 DAYS

BABY BROAD BEANS

Tender and tasty! Broad beans are beautiful! Really! A long time ago they were grown for their flowers not for their beans—now broad beans are beautiful again—this time on your plate! But—and this is a big, cruel BUT... you must eat them when they are only babies! Mmm... boiled baby broad beans... wicked!

You will need:

- **Small pots filled with soil**
- **Labels and waterproof pen**
- **Deeply dug garden soil, or a large container**
- **For tall varieties— garden netting or wire and several 3' (1 metre) canes**

Broad bean plants come in tall and dwarf varieties. The tall kind need to be tied onto netting to help them stand up, but the dwarf type can support themselves. In areas with mild Winters you can plant them in the Fall (Autumn), so they have a head start in the Spring, or you can sow them at the end of Winter, just before you plant all your other veggies. If you really, really love baby broad beans, you can just keep sowing them every six weeks to give you a constant supply.

1
Pop one bean in each pot filled with potting compost. Label and water well. Place your pots in a sunny windowsill. Water when you need to, not letting your plants get too wet or too dry.

2
When your plants have grown to about 3" (8 cm) tall and the weather is mild, it is time to plant them outside. Choose a sunny spot and dig in some compost and/or some well rotted manure.

3
Gently tap the bottoms of your pots and ease the plant into your hand. Plant your beans so they are at the same depth as they were in the pots.

4
Give your newly planted beans a good soaking—and remember to label the row with the date of transplanting and the name of the variety.

5
You can give yourself an extra treat when the plants reach their correct height by pinching off the top 2" (5 cm) of each plant. See page 77 for a yummy recipe. Pinching out the tops will also discourage blackflies, little sap-sucking insects who also enjoy bean tops.

6
Harvest your beans when the pods are about 6 to 8" (15 to 20 cm) long and the beans inside are still small. A big basket of broad bean pods doesn't give you very many little beans—but by gosh they are tasty little gems!

Don't worry if you missed a picking and you are left with bigger beans—all is not lost—it just means you have to double pod your beans—first take off the big furry jacket—boil them for 1 minute, let them cool, and then take off their undershirts!

14 WEEKS

NASTURTIUM LETTUCE ROSEMARY

FLIES

Boiled BB's p77

Beans on Toast p77

Beany Salad p77

Broad bean plants come in tall and dwarf varieties.

Broad beans must be eaten when they are only babies!

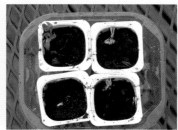

PLANTS = 4"
ROWS = 24"

7 DAYS

BEETROOTS

In the far off days of old, the roots of beets were used only as a medicine and it was the leaves that were prized as a vegetable. It was the good old Romans who changed the fortunes of the humble beet. Now the leaves and the roots are eaten and enjoyed in soups, stews, pickles and salads and, (shudder) even on your breakfast cereal!

You will need:

- A large, shallow container such as an apple or mushroom box
- Soil
- Seeds
- Labels and waterproof pen

1 Fill your container with soil to within ½" (1.5 cm) of the rim and firm it down well. Water the soil and let the water drain away.

2 Plant the beet seeds 2" (5 cm) apart each way by pushing them ½" (1.5 cm) into the soil. Water them in gently.

3 Place your beets somewhere warm and bright and water the compost whenever it dries out. Beetroot are tough little plants but the more care you give them the better crop you will have.

4 When your beetroots are the size of gobstoppers you can begin to harvest them… very carefully pull out every second one to leave them 4" (10 cm) apart. Fill the holes between the remaining beets with more soil and water the beets well. Let them grow to be larger beets or harvest them while they are still small.

Beets make a super food coloring. Try adding one small raw beetroot to your potatoes before you boil them up for mashing…. Grate it into the pan and boil your potatoes as normal. When the potatoes are cooked, drain and mash them up with a pat of butter… they will taste exactly the same as usual, but boy will they brighten up a dull dinner! You can also add a bit of beetroot to chopped apples before you make them into apple sauce to turn it a pretty pink.

By selecting the sweetest beets for many years, scientists developed the sugar beet. This sweet, white root now contains a whopping 20% sugar! The white stuff you put on your cereal may well come, not from sugar cane, but from beetroot! Sadly the beetroot that we can buy in the shops only has a measly 2% of sugar.

20%

In the 1800s beetroot juice was used as make-up to bring a rosy blush to a ladies' cheeks.

8–10 WEEKS

SUMMER-SAVOURY DILL

BIRDS FLIES

The Elizabethans in the sixteenth century were advised to wipe their beets with fresh dung before they cooked them. Mmmm, yummy!

Sunset Salad p78

Beetroot Brownies p78

Beetroot Jelly p78

Why did people dance to the vegetable band? Because it had a good beet!

PLANTS = 2"
ROWS = 12"

2 WEEKS

Have carrots always been orange? See page 95.

CARROTS

Carrots are easy-going and not at all fussy as long as the soil is crumbly and light. Given the right conditions they can grow super-quick to give crunchy slim roots for you to pull in only six to eight weeks! And carrots are hardy and not afraid of a bit of bad weather so they can be planted and placed outside right away.

You will need:

- **A container at least 12" (3 metres) wide and deep**
- **Soil**
- **Label and waterproof pen**
- **Seeds**

1
Choose your container—a bag, a box, a basket… what will it be? Prepare your label.

2
Fill with soil and kitchen compost to 1" (3 cm) of the rim of your container and water it well. Now sprinkle seeds thinly over the surface of the soil—remember each of those seeds is going to grow into a carrot so give them some room to develop. Sprinkle ¼" (0.5 cm) of soil on top of your seeds and water lightly.

3
Put your container in a sunny, sheltered spot and water when the surface of the compost dries out—in very hot or windy weather this may be twice a day. But only water if it's needed!

4
After several days the first leaves will appear and then it is time to start feeding your carrots with a weak plant food. Keep an eye on your carrots, feeding them weekly and watering them as necessary.

5
After six weeks, check to see if your carrots are ready by pulling out one or two. Grasp the feathery leaves down by the soil and pull gently.

Growing carrots in the garden is just as easy… just give them a good 'root run' and feed and water them every now and then. Prepare the soil by digging very deep. Heavy, hard to dig soils can be improved by adding lots of well rotted kitchen compost… and always remember to stay off heavy soils when they are wet. Carrots love an easy, loose soil to grow in; the long tap roots that we eat will grow short and dumpy if the soil is too hard and stony. Plant your carrots far enough apart so that you don't have to thin them. See the "know it all" section below. The main carrot pest, the carrot root fly, can smell the carrot seedlings when they are being pulled up. No thinning means fewer carrot root flies. Carrot root flies only fly a few inches above the ground so it's easy to stop them getting to your crop by putting something in their way. Try a fleecy barrier or a row of chives.

If you have somewhere warm and very bright you can even grow baby carrots inside in the middle of Winter.

6 WEEKS

ONIONS CHIVES GARLIC

CARROT FLIES

How do you turn soup into gold? Add 24 carrots!

400 years ago elegant ladies were advised to wear carrot fronds in their hats for decoration.

Rooty Tooty Soup p79

Orangey Carrot Muffins p79

Carroty Wraps p79

Can carrots really make you see in the dark or is this just an old wartime tale? See page 95.

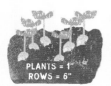

PLANTS = 1"
ROWS = 6"

2 WEEKS

How many other blue foods can you think of?

BLUEBERRIES

Blueberries are scrumptious and super-easy to grow, provided you give them what they like. They are rather fussy about the soil they grow in, but you can easily give them exactly what they need to keep them happy. Acid compost (called "ericaceous" compost) can be bought or you can even make your own.

You will need:

- A large pot
- Ericaceous compost
- Rainwater
- A blueberry plant

1 Choose a large pot, at least 15" (38 cm) deep and round. Fill it with a peat-free acid compost.

2 Soak your blueberry bush in rainwater for 20 minutes and plant it in its new pot to the same level, packing it in firmly.

3 Set up a bucket of water to catch the rain or use water from your water butt to water your blueberry—tap water is too alkaline (has too much lime in it) and will make your blueberry grow slowly and poorly. However tap water is better than no water!

4 Make a great tonic for acid-loving plants like your blueberries by saving old teabags and coffee grounds and soaking them in water. Give your blueberries a weak drink every week or so. Tea and coffee are acid and will help keep the soil acid. Feed your plant as you would others—but make sure you don't use tap water.

5 After two or three years your blueberry bush will need to be transplanted into a larger pot and you will need to prune your plant to keep it healthy and productive (making lots of fruit). This is very simple... just cut out 1/3 of all the branches down to the soil. First cut out any damaged branches, then choose the very oldest or thickest branches to prune out. And that's it!

You can make compost for your blueberry by filling a garbage bag with old pine bark and Fall (Autumn) leaves. Leave this mixture to rot down over the Winter and use it to top up your blueberry pot in the Spring.

Project—grow more blueberry plants to keep or give as gifts—turn to page 32 for easy instructions on how to take cuttings.

How many berries can one blueberry bush produce in one year? See page 95.

SAME YEAR

BIRDS

PLANTS = 5'
ROWS = 5'

Blueberry Crêpes p80

Blueberry Popsicles p80

what is
a ghost's
favorite
fruit?
Boo-berries!

Blueberry Pancakes p80

Bears love blueberries and they will travel for miles to find a blueberry patch.

How do you fix a flat pumpkin? with a pumpkin patch!

ZUCCHINI, PUMPKINS AND SQUASH

The squash family is a great big curious family which includes Halloween pumpkins, zucchini (courgettes), marrows, butternut and acorn squash and lots of others. All of them are easy to grow and, provided you give them lots of food and water, they can get to be a truly mammoth size. Both the female flowers, from which the fruit develop, and the larger male flowers that develop on the end of a thin stalk, are delicious to eat either cooked or torn and added to salads.

You will need:

- **Small pots filled with soil**
- **Seeds**
- **Labels and waterproof pen**

1 Plant one seed in each pot, 1" (3 cm) deep. Make sure the seed is on its side so that water doesn't collect on it and make it rot. Water your pots and place them in a warm, bright spot. As with other large seeds, you don't need to cover the soil with plastic.

2 Keep your plant well watered and well drained—seeds hate being soggy!—When the leaves appear move the plant to a sunny spot—but make sure it stays well watered!

3 When the weather begins to warm up and all danger of frost has passed, transplant your squash plants into the garden or into a large container. Dig a large hole and fill it with a mixture of soil, kitchen compost and/or well rotted manure and plant your seedling in the middle. Lay a thick layer of mulch around the plant but not touching the stem, and water it in well.

4 Keep on watering until your plant becomes established (begins to send roots down into the new soil). You can tell when this happens because all of a sudden it will put on a spurt of bright new growth.

5 Feed your squash plants every week all the way through the season (remember they are greedy) with an organic multi-purpose food (see page 11) or your own home-made plant food. If the weather is dry, give your plants a good drink… and always be on slug watch!

Keep on cutting! Zucchini (courgettes) will keep making new fruit (yep, they are a fruit!) as long as you keep on cutting. If you stop they'll think their job of making new seeds has finished and they will stop making fruit. And with all those delicious courgette recipes out there you don't want them to stop!!

10–24 WEEKS

BORAGE CALENDULA

SLUGS SNAILS MICE

Pumpkins—especially giant ones—need a very long growing season—start them off early and keep them very well fed and watered! Keep prize pumpkins off the soil by making them a bed of straw to sit on. Watch out for slugs and snails!

Summer squash, like zucchini (courgettes), are plants which are harvested early and have a soft skin. These don't store for a very long time but you get a lot of fruit from each plant. Cut this type when they are still small. Try carving your name in the top layer of skin in a small zucchini (courgette) and let it grow into a giant marrow—what happens?

Winter squash are plants with hard skins like pumpkins, butternut and acorn squash and gourds. These will store all through the Winter if they are kept in a cool, dry place. Turn them over every week to stop the underside bruising. Hard skinned squash have been used by fishermen, as floats to hold up their fishing nets, as pots, buckets and as lanterns.

Pumpkin Soup p81

Zucchini Dippers p81

Zucchini Fudge Cake p81

The worlds heaviest pumpkin to date weighed in at about 1,600 pounds... that's about the same as 22 average ten year olds!

PLANTS = 24"
ROWS = 24"

1 WEEK

CUCUMBER

You can grow bush cucumbers or climbing cucumbers and you can grow them in pots, up fences or in the veggie garden. They aren't difficult to grow; just choose the one that's right for you. There are greenhouse cucumbers that grow best in hot conditions and outdoor cucumbers (also called "ridge cucumbers") that will grow outside in cooler temperatures and still give you lots of fruit.

How much of a cucumber is water? 28%, 78% or 98%? See page 95.

You will need:

- **Small pots with drainage holes**
- **Soil**
- **Label and waterproof pen**
- **Seeds**
- **Popsicle sticks and plastic bag**

If you grow a climbing variety, have a look at the tendrils, which way do they twine, clockwise or anti-clockwise? Would they grow in the same direction if they were in the Southern Hemisphere? See page 95.

1 Fill a small pot with potting compost to ¼" (1cm) of the rim. Prepare your labels. Now plant your seeds, two per pot, ½" (1.5 cm) deep and water well. Cover with a plastic bag, held away from the soil by two popsicle sticks and place your pot in a warm bright space like a windowsill.

2 First the seed leaves will appear. If more than one seed has germinated, pinch out the rest of the seedlings to let the strongest grow. Feed and water your plant until it is warm enough to transplant outdoors.

3 Plant your cucumber in a large 14" (35 cm) pot filled with a mixture of soil and kitchen compost and/or well rotted manure. Mix in some water retaining crystals or seaweed crystals to help reduce the amount of watering you have to do.

4 OR dig a deep hole about 12 x 12" (30 x 30 cm) and fill it back up with soil mixed with kitchen compost or well rotted manure.

5 Supply a support if your want to train your climbing cucumbers to grow upwards or simply allow them to snake along the ground…. Bush cucumbers are well behaved and will stay in a tidy bush form so they don't need support or pinching cut.

6 Feed, feed, feed! Cucumbers, like squash and tomatoes, are very hungry plants and they will give you a magnificent crop if you remember to feed them with a high potash fertilizer every week… see page 11 for a recipe.

7 When several fruits have set, pinch out the end of the stem so the plant puts all its energy into ripening the fruit rather than growing bigger.

8 When your cucumbers are ready, ask an adult to cut them—the stalk is quite tough. Don't let them get too big or they will grow yellow and bitter—maybe like the kind the Egyptians dipped in honey!

12–14 WEEKS

BORAGE, DILL MARIGOLD BASIL

SLUGS SNAILS MICE

One Pot Dill Pickles p82

Cucumber Pinwheels p82

Tzatziki p82

Cucumbers have been grown in space! In 1982, Soviet astronauts grew cucumbers, radishes and lettuces in the space station above Earth.

Cucumbers have been grown for food for more than 3,000 years. That means they were eaten by, among others, the pyramid builders in Egypt (who ate them dipped in honey), the Romans and the Greeks.

PLANTS = 18"
ROWS = 18"

1 WEEK

CURRANTS AND GOOSEBERRIES

Desserts, puddings, jams and drinks... blackcurrants are famous for all the yummy recipes that can be made with them. But did you know that you can also grow redcurrants and whitecurrants? And their prickly friend, the good old gooseberry, is another super fruit to include in your patch.

You will need:

- **Healthy bushes**
- **Labels and waterproof pen**
- **Rich soil**
- **Mulch of well rotted manure**
- **Spade**
- **Secateurs**
- **Gloves... for gooseberries**

All these plants are great for growing anywhere in the garden—in amongst the flowers, in your veggie patch or in pots. If you grow them in pots, make sure the pot is really big... your bush will be in there for a long time.

The difference between the blackcurrants and the others is how you prune them— blackcurrants are grown as a bush with lots of stems coming out of the ground. Redcurrants, whitecurrants and gooseberries are all grown on a single trunk that sprouts lots of branches.

BLACKCURRANTS

Plant your new plant with the old soil mark 2" (5 cm) below ground. When your bushes are three or four years old, cut out ⅓ of the branches right down to ground level. Always cut out any dead, damaged or diseased shoots first, then choose the oldest, thickest branches to cut away.

REDCURRANTS, WHITECURRANTS AND GOOSEBERRIES

Redcurrants, white currants and gooseberries are all planted so the old soil mark on the stem is level with the ground. If any branches shoot up from the roots, cut them out. Prune the new growth by half in Winter... so, if a stem grew 4" (10 cm) in the last year, cut off 2". Simple! Always prune out any dead, diseased or damaged stems first.

All the currants and gooseberries like a rich soil with lots of organic matter like kitchen compost, and they all love a really good 2" blanket of mulch on the soil around their roots as well. If there is a dry spell of weather when the fruit is beginning to swell, be sure to give them a good drink!

Every Spring you should give your fruit bushes a good feed of slow release fertilizers and a new blanket of mulch.

Why did the gooseberry drown? Because the currants were too strong for him!

SAME YEAR

BIRDS

ROSEMARY FENNEL DILL

14,000 tonnes 🫐
= 3,000 🐘

over 14,000 tonnes of blackcurrants are grown in the UK each year. That's the same weight as 3,000 elephants!

Redcurrant Cupcakes p83

Gooseberry Fool p83

Blackcurrant Tart p83

PLANTS = 3'
ROWS = 5'

PEAS

Garden peas, sugarsnap peas, mange-tout and petit pois, marrowfat peas, mushy peas—more peas please!

You can grow dwarf peas which reach about 18" (45 cm) or tall peas that grow to more than a yard (metre). The shorter kind will begin to fruit sooner, but the taller kind will give you more peas to the row. Hmm… tricky decisions.

You will need to provide support for your peas by giving them something for them to climb up. Pea sticks are tall twiggy branches that are pushed into the ground to provide support for the growing peas. Peas cling on to their supports with tendrils that twist and curl around anything they touch. Don't be fooled by the delicate appearance of your young pea plants… when they grow up they will be very heavy and they can easily pull down netting or pea sticks which aren't sturdy enough.

You will need:

- **Small pots or egg boxes filled with soil**
- **Labels and waterproof pen**
- **Pea sticks or garden netting and stakes**

1
Peas need to be planted ½" (1.5 cm) deep and about 3" (8 cm) apart and the rows need to be about 16" (40 cm) apart.

2
You can start some peas off early by planting them in egg cartons. Fill the cups with soil and push the peas down into them with your finger. Label your seed trays with the name of the peas and the date you planted them and keep them well watered and in a warm, sunny spot.

3
Make new sowings indoors until the weather is warm enough for you to start sowing outside. When it is, you can do two jobs at once—plant your grown seedlings and making your next sowings of seeds.

4
Dig one trench for your oldest seedlings, another for your young seedlings and another for your seeds. First plant your row of the biggest seedlings, push the pea sticks in beside them. Do the same to the smaller

seedling, then plant your row of seeds. This way you will have a row beginning to crop just as the other one is finishing.

In mild areas, hardy wrinkled peas can be sown outside in the Fall (Autumn) so they can begin growing very early in the Spring. You could also try growing peas in containers for an easy-picking crop in a sunny spot on your patio. Some varieties have pretty flowers and pods that turn a delicate yellow.

10–16 WEEKS

SLUGS BIRDS MICE

PLANTS = 3" ROWS = 16"

Pasta and Peas p84

Cheesy Peasy Puffs p84

Mild Curry Pasties p84

A woman in Britain once ate 7,175 peas, one at a time, with chopsticks! It only took her one hour!

According to Norse legend, Thor, the thunder god, threw down a fistful of peas to punish his people. He meant them to clog up the wells, but some missed and sprouted instead.

7 DAYS

If Peter Piper picked a peck of pickled peppers, how many pickled peppers did Peter Piper pick? See page 95.

PEPPERS

Peppers are super veggies to grow in pots. They are warm weather plants that love a sun-baked spot, protected from cold winds and weather. There are red, yellow, green and even black and purple peppers and there are sweet peppers, hot peppers and tongue-on-fire peppers.

You will need:

- **Pepper seeds... there are zillions to choose from**
- **Small pots, such as yogurt pots**
- **Small plastic bags**
- **Popsicle sticks**
- **Soil**
- **Labels and waterproof pen**
- **A light-box, if needed (see above)**

If you have a greenhouse, cold frame or very sunny windowsill, that will be great. If not, try making a light-box by cutting away the sides of a medium-sized cardboard box and covering the inside with silver foil. This will increase the light that reaches your peppers and protect them from cold winds. If you are going to grow your peppers in this way, make sure you choose a variety which doesn't grow very tall!

1 Prepare your pots by filling with potting soil to ¼" (1 cm) of the rim and watering well. Pepper seeds are small and not many come in each packet of seeds so be careful when you're opening the packet.

2 Push one seed per pot ⅛" (3 mm) inch into the soil. Label your plant with the variety and date. Slip a plastic bag over the pot and hold it away from the soil with two popsicle sticks pushed down the sides.

3 Place your pots in a warm spot... peppers germinate best at a temperature of about 85° F (29° C). Water as necessary... don't let them become too dry or too soggy. When your seeds germinate remove the plastic bag to increase the air flow around them.

4 When the roots begin to show in the holes in the bottom of your pots, it is time to transplant your peppers to their permanent homes. Fill the new larger pot with soil and make a hole in the soil the size of the small pot. Gently ease your pepper plant out by tapping the base of the upturned pot. Be careful not to handle it by the stem... if the stem is damaged your plant will die, but if a leaf is damaged your plant can grow a new one.

5 Settle your pepper into its new home by gently firming the soil around the roots and giving it a good drink of weak fertilizer. If you are growing your plant inside you won't

15 WEEKS

BORAGE CALENDULA

SLUGS SNAILS FLIES

Pepper Pots p85

Pepper and Halloumi Skewers p85

want to use nettle or comfrey soup to feed it… too stinky! Choose instead an organic tomato fertilizer and remember to feed your peppers once a week.

Harvest your peppers by cutting the stem close to where it grows from the branch. If you keep your peppers inside be extra careful not to get any water on the leaves or fruit because the water drops will act like a magnifying glass with the sun and burn your plant.

If you move your plant outside remember to let it get used to the stronger sunshine and cooler nights of its outdoor home by putting it out for a few hours to begin with and bringing it in at night. Each day increase the time it spends outside and by the end of one week it will be tough enough to stay outside.

The Aztec people of Central and South America began growing chillies more than 7,000 years ago. By the time the Spanish explorers sailed up to their 'shores' the Aztecs were eating chilli peppers with their hot chocolate.

When is a hot vegetable not a hot vegetable? When it's a chilli!

In india hot and spicy chilli peppers are hung over the doorway to ward off evil spirits.

PLANTS = 12"
ROWS = 24"

14 DAYS

SACK OF POTATOES

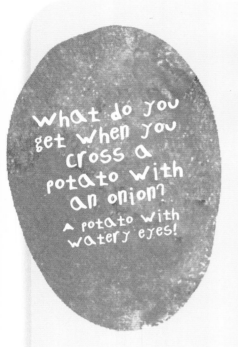

What do you get when you cross a potato with an onion?
A potato with watery eyes!

How many different kinds of potato are there? Have a look in the supermarket next time you go shopping. There are waxy potatoes and floury potatoes and they come in pink, yellow, purple and blue, as well as the usual white and brown. There are sweet little baby potatoes and great, big, enormous potatoes. People have written whole books, just about potatoes, and potatoes have changed the history of entire countries. And you thought that potatoes were just potatoes!

You will need:

• **One large or several small containers, at least 2' (60 cm) deep. You can use pots, barrels, large baskets or even heavy-duty bags or sacs with drainage holes poked into the bottom**

• **Rich soil with plenty of well rotted manure or kitchen compost added**

• **Labels and waterproof pen**

You can grow them in the garden or in containers… either way they need the same growing conditions and care.

Early or 'new' potatoes need to be 'chitted' to give them a head start by helping them to begin growing very early in the year. Buy 'first early' potatoes in Spring and lay them out in an egg box or a tray in a warm, bright spot inside. Set them out, not touching each other, with their knobbly eyes pointing up. They don't need any soil at this stage and you don't need to water them or do anything else. When strong green shoots have sprouted it's time to plant them in their proper home. **Main crop potatoes** can be planted without chitting.

1
Fill the bottom of the pot with a 4" layer of soil and set the potatoes with their shoots or eyes pointing up and about 6" apart.

2
Completely cover the potatoes with another 4 to 6" (10 to 12 cm) of soil and firm it around them gently being careful not to damage the growing shoots. Do this each time the shoots reappear until you reach the top of your pot. This is called earthing up.

3
Allow the shoots to grow big and strong. Feed your potatoes with an organic fertilizer that is high in potash, like the nettle or comfrey soup on page 11.

4
After several weeks your potatoes will begin to flower. You can harvest small new potatoes when the flowers just begin to appear. For larger potatoes wait for the flowers to fade, then tip the container out (use newspaper or plastic to stop the soil going everywhere) and examine your treasures.

Plant some potatoes in August or September and leave the pot in a sheltered, sunny place like a porch or greenhouse to harvest potatoes for Christmas!

10–14 WEEKS

SLUGS WORMS

PLANTS = 12"
ROWS = 24"

Rosti p86

Frittata p86

Potato Wedges p86

In Ireland in the 1840s, a dreadful disease attacked the potato crop. Year after year the fungus disease attacked the potatoes and year after year the people of Ireland watched as their crops rotted in the fields. The people grew weaker and poorer. Over one million people died and two million were forced to leave their homes and their country forever. In those days plant diseases weren't properly understood.

Seed potatoes—which aren't seeds at all—are potatoes which are grown in a place where no diseases can infect them so there isn't another disaster like the one that devastated Ireland.

Only the tuber—the potato itself—is edible. All other parts; the leaves, flowers and fruit of the potato are poisonous. 400 years ago when potatoes were first brought over from South America, Queen Elizabeth's cooks took one look at the ugly roots and threw them out. Unfortunately, they kept the poisonous stems and leaves, cooked them and served them up to their queen and her friends at a banquet. Boy, were they in trouble!

Green potatoes are also poisonous…
keep your spuds in the dark to stop them going green.

6 WEEK

RASPBERRIES

Raspberries are ridiculous! All they want to do is to grow and give you lots of luscious berries and there is almost nothing you can do to stop them! Raspberries are produced on thorny vines and we grow them by planting canes (rooted sticks) and training them onto fences or wires. Almost anyone can grow raspberries, almost anywhere, because they are tough and hardy. They will even grow in troughs on a high-rise balcony.

Raspberries are an important bee crop.

You will need:

- **Raspberry canes**
- **Nylon string or garden wire**
- **Sturdy posts, 6 to 8' (2 metres) tall**
- **Lots of well rotted manure and/ or kitchen compost**
- **Hammer and spade**
- **Gloves**

1 Choose your spot. Your raspberries will be growing in the same spot for many years so you'll need to dig deeply and add lots of lovely muck and kitchen compost to your planting holes. Raspberries don't like wet feet so the ground must be well-drained. Dig a long narrow strip to encourage your raspberries to grow in a well behaved row.

2 Plant your canes about 18" (45 cm) apart, and at the same depth as the old soil mark on the cane.

3 Water them very well.

4 Fall (Autumn) fruiting varieties are shorter and sturdier than others so you don't need to use stakes or wires (though this may help in windy sites). Early and late Summer types need to be trained and tied onto sturdy supports.

5 Hammer two (or more for longer rows) 6 to 8' (2 metres) posts into the ground 10' (3 metres) apart. Tie nylon string or wire between the posts at even distances.

6 Tie your raspberries to the wires, spreading them out to make picking easier later on. As they grow, keep tying them in and water when necessary—when they have grown lots of new roots you won't need to water them unless the weather is very dry.

7 Prune your Summer raspberries after they have finished fruiting. Cut down all the old canes that gave you fruit this season. You will easily be able to tell the difference. Leave the new, unfruited canes and tie them onto the wires ready to give you lots of luscious berries next year! Prune your Fall raspberries by cutting down all the canes to ground level in late Winter.

8 Feed and mulch your plants in early Spring and then add a good deep layer of well rotted manure and/or kitchen compost.

You can grow early, mid-season or Fall raspberries. And if you really love raspberries you can grow all three.

Not all raspberries are red... they come in black, yellow and orange too.

SAME YEAR

DILL FENNEL

BIRDS

Space scientists have discovered that the dust clouds that swirl around in our galaxy, the Milky way, actually taste of raspberries.

Raspberry Fizz p87

One Pot Jam p87

Summer Pudding p87

Raspberries were collected on the slopes of Mount Ida near the city of Troy.

PLANTS = 18"
ROWS = 3"

RHUBARB

The lovely long red stems of rhubarb are grown from 'crowns', solid clumps which sprout roots from the bottom and leaves and flowers from the top. Rhubarb comes back year after year and because it will grow in the same place for a long time it is important to give it a lovely, rich soil in full sun. Once you have planted rhubarb you really don't need to do anything to it at all except to give it a good blanket of mulch in the Spring and in the Fall (Autumn). Rhubarb is a great plant to pop into the corner of the flower garden.

You will need:

• A sharp spade

• Lots of rich compost or well rotted manure

Plants can be bought from any garden center but if you know someone who grows rhubarb they may let you have a piece of their plant. Here's how to divide a crown of rhubarb.

1 Lift the rhubarb out of the ground by digging up the whole crown. This is easiest to do in the Fall (Autumn) when the leaves have died away.

2 Slice a section off the side of the crown, making sure it has both roots and the knobbly growths at the top from where leaves have grown.

3 Replant the original crown back into its hole and give it a good mulch of well rotted manure to settle it back in and give it a good boost.

4 Dig a new hole for your new piece of rhubarb crown about twice as big as the crown itself. Mix the soil with plenty of well-rotted manure and replace it into the hole.

5 Plant your rhubarb into this rich crumbly bed, making sure you place it so the soil is at the same level as it was before. Firm the soil around the crown so there are no pockets of air that may fill with water and freeze solid in the Winter—no plants like ice-cubes around their roots!

6 Finish off by giving your rhubarb a blanket of mulch about 2" (5 cm) deep. Leave a space in the middle so the mulch doesn't touch the crown, which may cause it to rot.

7 In the Spring, when the first leaves just begin to sprout, you can encourage your plant to grow tender early stems by keeping it in the dark. Place a very large pot upside-down over the crown—this will make the plant send up long slim stalks, searching for the light in late Winter.

8 Harvest your rhubarb by grasping a stem close down to where it emerges from the crown. Pull and twist the stem at the same time and, mmm, enjoy!

6 MONTHS

SLUGS
SNAILS

PLANTS = 3'
ROWS = 3'

Rhubarb can be 'forced' by putting a pot over the crown to encourage it to grow tender pale stems early in the year. Clay forcing pots are prized by gardeners.

Marco polo introduced rhubarb to the West, when he brought it back with him after his adventures in China....

Rhubarb leaves are poisonous to eat, but they make a great addition to the compost heap.

Rhubarb has been grown and used for about 5,000 years, but it is only in the last 200 years that it has been enjoyed as a food… before that it was used as a medicine to cure tummy aches.

Rhubarb Sundae p88

Rhubarb Flapjacks p88

Rhubarb Crumble p88

SALADINGS... CUT AND COME AGAIN

Lettuce is what we usually think of as our salad veg, but there isn't just one kind of lettuce... there are loads. And there are many other leafy greens that we can easily grow to add to salads to make them tasty and colorful.

You will need:

- Containers or a garden space
- Light soil, or a patch of well dug garden soil
- Labels and waterproof pen

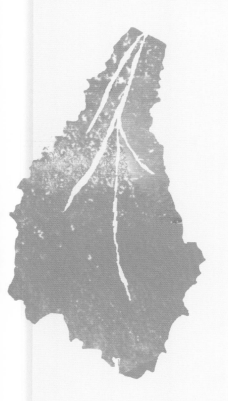

Lettuces are often grown in identical rows, but there is another way. Even in a tiny space you can grow 'cut and come again' salad made of a mixture of different leaves that you can keep picking and pruning. They will go on and on supplying you with salad plants to go in sandwiches and to eat with eggs, pasta, pizza, quiche, mmm....

1 Choose a space, either in your garden or a container—troughs or shallow tubs are just right.

2 Dig over the soil until it's very fine and crumbly (or fill your container with good potting soil to ¼" (6 mm) of the rim.) Lettuce seeds, and the seeds of other saladings are tiny and they need to be planted on the surface of fine soil. Rake the top of the soil until it's flat.

3 Sprinkle your seed evenly over the surface of the soil, so that there are no large spaces left bare—leave about 1" (2 to 3 cm) between the seeds—but don't worry about the spacing—you can pull up the seedlings which are too close together. Sprinkle a dusting of fine soil over the seeds, so they are ever so slightly covered. Water in well, using a watering can with a fine rose or use your seed sprinkler. Be very gentle—you don't want to wash the seeds

down into the soil or into a clump at the corner of your patch! Lettuce doesn't like to be too hot... germination will be poor if the temperature is too high.

4 Keep an eye on your patch to make sure that it doesn't dry out and that your growing seedlings are not devoured by the dreaded slug! Thin any overcrowded seedlings as they emerge—use your thinnings in sandwiches.

5 When your plants are about 5 to 6" (12 to 15 cm) tall you can start cutting them—pick a few leaves from the outside of each plant—never take the middle leaves because these are the growing tips and your plants won't be able to put on any new growth if the growing tips are damaged.

2 WEEKS

CHIVES FENNEL

SLUGS SNAILS

A box or pot of home-grown salad leaves is a quick and easy gift to grow for any adult. Choose leaf lettuces, purslane, herb mixes, beetroot, spring onions or a ready-mixed packet of 'cut and come again' leaves.

Lettuce juice has been used to cure scorpion bites, poor eyesight and "wamblings of the stomach"!

In World War Two, hospitals used a medicine made from wild lettuce to sooth patients to sleep. The Ancient Greeks also knew lettuce could soothe people to sleep, so they served it at the end of a meal. But the mean Emperor Domitian used to have it served at the beginning of his feasts so he could torture his guests by making them stay awake in his presence!

In France, 400 years ago, lettuce hearts were candied and eaten as a food called "Angels Throats".

Emperor Caesar Augustus of Rome erected a statue praising lettuce because he believed eating it had cured him of an illness!

Super Salad Scooby Snack p89

Salmon Caesar Salad p89

Flower Power Salad p89

PLANTS = 1"
ROWS = 1"

1 WEEK

Why did the baby strawberry cry?

Because his parents were in a jam!

STRAWBERRIES

Summertime is strawberry time. Strawberries enjoy a good rich soil, with lots of added compost, and they like sun and moisture too. But don't worry if you have a partly shady spot because they will still work hard to give you a good crop... even in hanging baskets. One plant can give you almost half a pound of strawberries!

You will need:

- A sharp spade
- Strawberry plant, at least one year old
- Pot of soil
- A peg made from sturdy bent wire
- Scissors
- Labels and waterproof pen

To grow strawberries by layering is simple... the plant does all the work—it even plants itself. All you have to do is supply the pot.

1
Choose a strawberry plant that is sending out long, flexible stems called "runners". At the end of each runner a new baby plant will grow.

2
Fill a pot with soil and bury it in the ground close to the mother plant. Water the soil well.

3
Hold the end of the runner into the pot of soil using a peg made from a piece of sturdy wire.

4
Water your growing plantlet when needed—often when the weather is dry and warm—and wait for it to develop roots and put on new top growth. At the warm height of Spring this could be in as little as two weeks!

5
When you think your plantlet has grown into a proper plant, give it a gentle tug—if it resists you know your plant has rooted and you can cut the stem that links it to the mother plant.

6
Now it is time to settle your plant into its new home. Do this by planting it in full sun or part-shade in a generous hole filled with a mixture of soil and kitchen compost or well-rotted manure. Mulch around your plant with straw or shredded bark to keep the roots moist and slugs away from your ruby jewels!

Surprisingly, a very good mulch around strawberry plants is—guess what?—straw!

Strawberries are a slugs favorite tea-time treat. A great way to beat the slugs is to grow your strawberries in hanging baskets. Choose the largest basket you can—strawberries don't like to be dry and it is easier to keep them moist in a large basket. Fill the basket with a mixture of soil, kitchen compost and a sprinkling of water retaining crystals. These will make all the difference in the warmth of Summer. Sink a quart (½ litre) drinks bottle half way into the compost to make watering easier. A large hanging basket will happily hold four strawberry plants.

SAME YEAR

MARIGOLDS ONIONS CHIVES

SLUGS BIRDS

Strawberry Trifle p90

Strawberry Shake p90

Strawberry Shortcake p90

How do you make a strawberry shake? Take him to a scary movie!

In parts of Germany, small baskets of wild strawberries are tied to cows' horns in Spring as an offering to elves. Tradition says that in return the elves, who love strawberries, will help to look after the animals.

PLANTS = 18"
ROWS = 18"

How many seeds are inside a strawberry? See page 95.

SUNFLOWERS

Sunflowers are the sunny giants of the veggie patch, often growing to more than 10' (3 metres) (that is the height of a very tall person standing on the shoulders of another very tall person!). Sunflowers also give you seeds to roast and munch on, seeds to save for the birds, and— not many people know this—a tasty, crunchy vegetable. The flower buds, before they open, can be picked and stir-fried to make a deliciously different meal.

You will need:

- **Sunflower seeds**
- **Medium-sized pots such as tin cans with holes punched in the bottom**
- **Soil**
- **Organic plant food**
- **Labels and waterproof pen**
- **Large tub filled with soil**
- **Tall bamboo canes**
- **Soft string**

Sunflowers come in all shapes and sizes— from dwarf plants that produce masses of flowers on one plant to enormously tall specimens that only have 1 very large flower each.

You can start your plants off early in the year by planting them in medium-sized pots indoors or you can plant them directly outside in pots or in the garden when the weather has warmed up.

1
To start them off early, plant your sunflower seeds one per pot and tuck the seeds 1" (3 cm) deep into the soil. Water them in well and place them in a bright spot to grow. You want your plant to grow strong and sturdy—especially if you are growing a giant—so make sure you give it the sunniest spot you can find.

2
First the seed leaves will appear, followed quickly by the true leaves. Soon your sunflowers will be ready to transplant into their proper home. Choose a sunny, well-dug corner of the garden or a really large tub (the bigger the better) to grow your sunflowers in—a larger tub will be sturdier and hold more water and nutrients than a small one.

3
Feed your plant every time you water with an organic plant food. If they are in a windy spot you may need to stake your plant with a very tall, sturdy bamboo cane pushed very deeply into the ground. If you

are growing it in a container, you will have to tie the cane to a railing, gutter pipe or other fixed object—it would be sad if your giant fell over and was damaged. Use soft string to secure the stem to the cane.

4
Slugs are just as keen on sunflowers as birds are so make sure you keep a keen eye out for glistening slug and snail trails and dispose of the little critters before they dispose of your plant!

5
In damp climates cut the head when the seeds are visible but the ray petals are still on the flower and hang the flower heads upside-down in a covered, draughty spot to dry. In hot dry climates your sunflowers can be left to dry where they grow.

If you are growing a patch of sunflowers for the birds you can either leave the plants standing or cut and hang the heads upside down in the garden where the birds will find them.

15–20 WEEKS

SQUASH CLIMBING BEANS

SLUGS

There can be over 200 seeds on a single sunflower head! The oil that can be squeezed from these seeds is used to fry chips in the kitchen... and as fuel to power cars and trucks!

Sunflowers track the sun across the sky. In the morning they face East to greet the rising sun. Throughout the day they follow the sun across the sky until, by evening, all the flowers in the patch are facing West. Overnight the flower heads slowly turn eastwards again so they are ready to greet the sun at dawn.

How tall was the tallest sunflower in the world? Was it 12 feet, 18 feet, 25 feet or 68 feet tall? See page 95.

PLANTS = 12"
ROWS = 24"

2 WEEKS

CORN

To grow corn you must first decide if you want baby corn, corn on the cob or popcorn. They all come from completely different kinds of corn plants.

Corn is wind pollinated, so the wind must be able to blow the pollen about between the corn plants to have the best chance of pollinating all the kernels and to allow them to grow into plump, sweet cobs. That is why sweet corn and popcorn are always planted in groups, rather than rows.

Baby corn, however, is eaten before the cobs are pollinated so it can be planted anywhere; one by one along the back of a row of flowers or in little groups or even in pots.

1
Plant your corn kernels (seeds) five to a 5" (13 cm) pot, filled with good potting compost. Push them 1" (3 cm) into the soil. Water well and place on a sunny windowsill.

2
Grow these until they are 3" tall. Keep watering them when they need it and turn them while they grow to make sure they all grow tall and strong.

3
Prepare your ground outside by digging it over very well and digging it deeply. Add as much compost as you can… corn is a hungry plant. Now plant your corn plants 15" (38 cm) apart each way. Plant them firmly, water them in and firm them in again.

4
When your plants are about 12" (30 cm) tall, carefully mulch around them with 3 or 4" (10 cm) of rich compost and water them again.

5
When the corn plants have reached their mature height the male flowers will grow from the top of the stalk and the female flowers, looking like tassels of silk, will grow from the top of each immature corn cob on the stem. When there is no wind you can help the pollen on its journey by giving the male flowers a gentle shake… if the time is right you will be able to see the pollen fall, like grains of dust, down to the silky pollen tubes.

6
Harvest the cobs in late Summer when the silks have turned brown and withered.

Seeds labelled 'supersweet' are the best for eating as corn on the cob and corn kernels because they are so high in sugar. The sugar begins to decline just 20 minutes after picking so eat your corn fresh!

Sweet corn has no popability—popcorn is a different variety of corn and if you want to grow both you must grow them at least 20' (6 metres) away from each other, otherwise the corn and the popcorn will cross-pollinate and will produce a tough kernel which won't pop properly.

You must grow your corn in a block instead of a single row—a group of corn plants at least four plants by four plants is best… more is better!

You will need:

- **Medium-sized pots, such as old fruit punnets or large yogurt pots**
- **Soil**
- **Lots of well-rotted manure or kitchen compost**
- **Labels and waterproof pen**

14 WEEKS

CLIMBING BEANS
LETTUCE
SQUASH

SQUIRRELS
MICE
SLUGS

Corn Fritters p91

BBQ Corn p91

Corn Relish and
Toasted Halloumi p91

Why did the
corn get mad
at the farmer?
Because he
Kept pulling
his ears!

PLANTS = 15"
ROWS = 15"

2 WEEKS

TOMATOES

The evil tomato—in the olden days people believed that tomatoes would give them nasty diseases and, while the Aztecs grew and ate tomatoes, it took more than 200 years before the rest of the world followed their example.

Everyone knows, don't they, that tomatoes are red… yellow, orange, purple, striped, round, square, pointed, oval, knobbly, tiny and huge. Well, at least, unlike the people of old, we all know that tomatoes are delicious!

There are two types of tomato plant; **bush** and **cordon**. Bush tomatoes are neat and well-behaved and they don't need pruning. You can get very small bush tomatoes that will easily fit three plants in a hanging basket, or big bush toms that will fill a 14" pot.

Cordon tomatoes grow like climbing vines. They need a bit more care but they aren't tricky, once you know to pinch off the little side-shoots that grow from between the leaf and the stem.

Tomato farmers employ bumble bees to work in their greenhouses to fertilize their crops.

You will need:

- **A tomato plant**
- **A large pot filled with soil**
- **Plant food (lots!)**
- **Bamboo cane and soft twine**
- **Label and waterproof pen**

1 Choose your tomato plant—bush or cordon? Tiny toms or massive monsters? Place your baby plant in its pot in the sunniest indoor spot that you have and turn it daily so that it doesn't grow crookedly towards the sun.

2 To begin with, you want to encourage your new plant to grow a good, strong set of roots and healthy leaves. Feed it every time you water it with a weak fertilizer, made up to only ½ strength.

3 With all the feeding, warmth and care you give it, your baby plant will soon outgrow its small pot. Choose a new pot that will fit the final size of your tomato plant. Some small trailing bush plants can be planted three to a hanging basket, while larger varieties will need a deep pot at least 15" (40 cm) wide.

4 Transplant your tomato into its new home and sink a thick bamboo cane firmly into the pot. Tie the stem to the cane with soft twine.

5 If you grow small bush toms outside you can increase the light and warmth by growing them in a light box… see the peppers page for how to make one.

6 If you are growing a cordon, you must keep on pinching out the little side shoots that grow from between the main stem and the leaf. If you let these grow your plant will put all its growing energy into making more and more leaves instead of giving you lots of luscious tomatoes. Once the main stem has reached its proper height you need to stop it growing any taller by cutting off the top of the main stem. A bush plant only needs to be tied to a cane if it grows too big and heavy to support itself. Once the

15–20 WEEKS

MARIGOLDS PARSLEY BASIL

FLIES

Tomato and Feta Salad p92

Cheese and Tomato Tart p92

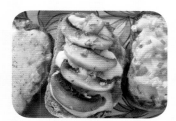

Pizza/Pasta Sauce p92

first flowers appear you need to switch to a high potash fertilizer—good old nettle and comfrey soup is ideal (see page 11) if you are growing outside, but it is far too stinky for inside. Use an organic tomato food and feed your plants every week until the very end of the season.

7 Tomatoes taste better if they are not kept in the fridge. Store your tomatoes in a warm bright room out of direct sunlight. At the end of the year if you have too many green tomatoes you can ripen a few by putting them in a paper bag along with a banana. Bananas produce ethylene gas, the same gas that scientists use to ripen tasteless commercial tomatoes.

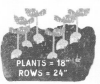

PLANTS = 18"
ROWS = 24"

2 WEEKS

What color were tomatoes 500 years ago? See page 95.

The tallest tomato plant on record was 28 feet tall. That is the same as a seven ordinary ten year olds standing on each others shoulders.

HERBS

Herbs are an essential part of all gardens. They add flavor and color and scent and they do a wonderful job of encouraging the garden good guys and controlling the bad.

MINT
(perennial, grow from cuttings or division)

There are many different mints, all with their own scent and flavor. Spearmint (garden mint) is the type we use to make mint sauce. It is a very quick grower and will quickly spread around the garden, popping up all over the place. Plant it in a bottomless pot sunk into the ground—where it will get the moisture and nutrients it needs but its invasive roots won't spread. Apple mint and pineapple mint are pretty, variegated plants that have a fruity scent and flavor. They're nice in fruit salads and sorbets and fruity drinks! Chocolate mint is quite different—it really does taste and smell just like a minty chocolate bar. Add a couple of leaves to hot chocolate for a special treat!

PARSLEY
(biennial, grow from seed)

Start them off in small pots (yoghurt pots are great) and transplant seedlings to the garden, to larger pots or into hanging baskets. Super in salads, sauces and always with garlic.

BASIL
(annual, grow from seed or transplant supermarket basil)

Basil likes hot weather and plenty of sun. The lovely flavor is perfect with pasta and tomatoes.

DILL
(annual, grow from seed)

Dill is a lovely, scented herb to grow; it looks pretty among flowers and it's nice to walk past and trail your fingers through its scented, feathery fronds. Dill leaves are delicious chopped up finely in potato salads and dill seed is perfect for adding to sweet vinegar to pickle baby cucumbers— give it a go!

MARJORAM AND OREGANO
(perennial, grow from division)

There are many different types and some are very pretty as well as tasty. Keep on pinching the tips and don't forget you can use the flowers too. Essential in spaghetti sauce and pizzas!

THYME
(perennial, grow from cuttings)

Thyme makes a lovely edging plant and is super in hanging baskets. There are more than 400 kinds of thyme… even one that smells exactly like lemon sherbet. They are all delicious in cooked dishes and salads.

LAVENDER
(perennial, grow from cuttings)

Lavender flowers are so sweetly scented that many people don't think of them as food, but they are perfect in puddings, jellies and ice-cream. Trim it every year to keep it tidy and healthy.

ROSEMARY
(perennial, grow from cuttings and layering)
Rosemary comes in all sorts of scents and flavors, even ginger. Add this one to tomato sauce and stews and roasted Winter veggies.

CHIVES
(perennial, grow from seed or division)
Chives attract bees, ward off pests, add their own flavor and mimic the flavor of onions or garlic. And, of course, they are very pretty too. Add the flowers and the leaves to cooked or cold dishes.

FENNEL
(annual, grow from seed)
There is a green type and a very beautiful bronze type that will fit nicely in the veggie or flower garden. The leaves, chopped finely, are scrummy in drinks, with fish, and—mmm, the best—with potato salad.

CALENDULA
(annual, grow from seed)
The bright orange and yellow petals of calendula make a delightful splash in a salad and add color and flavor to Summer soups. You can even make a tea with it.

SAGE
(perennial, grow from cuttings or layering)
Sage is a great partner for lemony flavors, with onions in stuffings and sauces. Sage has a great depth of flavor which adds extra oomph to stews—but beware; don't add too much because it is very strong.

LEMON BALM
(perennial, grow from cuttings or division)
The yellow splashed variegated balm is another touchy-feely herb that is fun to have near a path or seat. Brush your hand over the leaves and you will be surrounded by the scent of sugary lemons. Use lemon balm in hot and cold drinks. Chop finely in salads and use to decorate ice-creams and puddings.

NASTURTIUMS
(annual, grow from seed)
Both the leaves and the flowers are edible, with a sharp peppery flavor. Choose small leaves and the individual petals of flowers in salads and sandwiches.

Herby Scones p93

Minty Ice-Cream p93

Alphabet Soup p93

RECIPES

GARLICKY BEANS

- 1lb (450 g) tender green beans of any kind
- 2 cloves garlic, minced
- 1 tablespoon butter or butter and olive oil mixed
- Sea salt

1 Leave small beans whole or cut larger beans into 2" (5 cm) lengths.

2 Cook the beans in boiling, salted water for 3 minutes, until just tender. Drain very well and return to the pan.

3 Add the butter and garlic to the beans and leave to cook gently for another 3 minutes, until there is no squeak left. Cover and set aside until ready to serve.

BEANY BURGERS

- 6 tablespoons olive oil
- 1 onion, very finely chopped
- 1 clove garlic, minced
- 1 tablespoon parsley, chopped
- ½ teaspoon each of chopped rosemary and marjoram
- ½ teaspoon cumin
- 2 cups shelled beans, cooked
- 2 tablespoons fresh breadcrumbs
- 1 egg, beaten

1 Heat 2 tablespoons of the oil in a frying pan, add the onions and garlic, cover with a lid and cook on a medium heat until soft and lightly golden.

2 Add the herbs and cook for one minute.

3 In a bowl, mash the beans with a potato masher, then add the onion mixture, the breadcrumbs and the egg and mix well.

4 Divide the mixture into four, roll each portion into a ball and flatten them with the palm of your hand.

5 Heat the remaining olive oil in the frying pan over a medium heat. Cook your burgers for 5 minutes each side or until browned.

6 Serve in a bun, topped with lettuce and sliced tomatoes.

CHILLI BEAN WRAPS

- Small tub garlic and herb cream cheese
- 4 soft flour tortillas
- 1 ½ cups shelled beans, cooked
- ¼ teaspoon chilli powder
- 1 teaspoon paprika
- 1 tablespoon red or yellow pepper, chopped finely

1 Roughly mash ½ the beans and combine with the rest of the ingredients and the remaining beans.

2 Spread the cream cheese over the tortilla wraps.

3 Top the cream cheese with the bean mixture.

4 Roll the wraps up to make a sausage shape. Serve with coleslaw or salad.

BOILED BB'S

- 1lb (450 g) shelled baby broad beans
- pinch of salt

The best and the easiest way to serve broad beans is simply to boil them while they are still babies and serve them piping hot. Don't forget that broad bean tips (the tender tops of each plant) are a delicacy. You wont be able to buy in the shops.

BEANS ON TOAST

- 1lb (450 g) baby broad beans
- 2 spring onions, sliced
- 2 cloves garlic, minced
- tiny pinch of crushed chilli flakes
- scant tablespoon of chopped coriander
- 2 tablespoons good olive oil
- 4 large, thick slices of very good fresh bread
- 3 oz (85 g) shaved parmesan cheese

1 Boil the baby broad beans in until just tender; about 3 minutes. Drain and keep warm.

2 Heat the oil in a frying pan over a medium heat and cook the spring onions and garlic for 5 minutes. Add the chilli flakes and the broad beans and cook for 2 minutes. Remove from the heat and stir in the coriander. Cover and keep warm.

3 Toast the bread and place on warmed serving plates. Spoon the bean mixture over the toasts and serve with a dish of grated cheese.

BEANY SALAD

- 3 bean salad
- 1 cup broad beans
- 1 cup green beans, sliced into 1 inch pieces
- 1 tin chick peas, drained
- 4 tablespoons olive oil
- 2 tablespoons wine vinegar
- 1 teaspoon sugar
- 1 tablespoon chopped fresh parsley
- 2 tablespoons chopped fresh mixed herbs

1 Cook the broad beans in slightly salted water for 3 minutes or until just tender. Drain and cool.

2 Cook the green beans in slightly salted water for 2 minutes, or until just tender. Drain, mix with the broad beans and cool. Drain and rinse the chickpeas and add to the beans.

3 Mix the remaining ingredients together in a screw topped jar, shake vigorously until the sugar has dissolved and pour the dressing over the bean mixture. Refrigerate to allow the flavors to develop.

4 Serve at room temperature accompanied by crusty bread.

BEETROOT JELLY

- 4 cooked beetroot, grated
- 1 apple, peeled and grated
- 1 crisp pear, peeled and grated
- 1 pint strawberry or raspberry jelly
- Oil

1 Very lightly oil a 1 pint (500 ml) shallow dish.

2 Make up the jelly and pour into the shallow dish. Add the beetroot, apple and pear. Stir to distribute the beetroot and fruit evenly around the dish. Refrigerate until set.

3 Serve along with other salads or as a pudding on its own.

BEETROOT BROWNIES

- 10 oz (285 g) melted dark chocolate
- 10 oz (285 g) melted butter
- 10 oz (285 g) sugar
- 3 eggs, beaten
- 6 oz (170 g) self-raising flour
- 8 oz (225 g) cooked beetroot, peeled and grated

1 Put the grated beetroot in a colander to drain.

2 Preheat the oven to 350° F (180° C). Grease a 8 x 10" (20 x 25 cm) cake tin and line the bottom with baking paper.

3 Mix chocolate and butter together.

4 Cream the eggs and sugar together in a bowl until light and fluffy. Add the chocolate mixture and stir until smooth.

5 Fold in the flour, then the beetroot and stir until it is just mixed.

6 Pour the mixture into the cake tin and bake in the oven for about 30 minutes or until a knife pushed into the middle comes out clean.

SUNSET SALAD

- 2 oranges, washed
- 5 small beetroot, washed

1 Cut the leaves off the beetroot, but don't cut into the root at all or the juice will run away while they are being cooked. Cook the beetroot in boiling water until tender, about ½ an hour. Cool.

2 Cut the stump of leaves from the top of the beetroot. Slip the skins off and discard. Cut into ¼" (1 cm) chunks and place in a serving bowl.

3 Cut the skin from the top and bottom of the oranges. Rest one orange on the bottom surface, cut away the skin by sawing down between the skin and the flesh. Cut the flesh into ¼" pieces, removing the pips and as much as the bitter white pith as possible.

4 Do the same to half of the other orange. With the remaining half, do not remove the skin, instead cut the whole thing into smaller pieces, skin and all.

5 Toss the oranges together with the beetroot and leave for an hour or two for the flavors to develop.

ROOTY TOOTY SOUP

- 1lb (450 g) carrots, chopped
- 1 medium onion, chopped
- 1 medium parsnip, chopped
- 1 medium potato, chopped
- 1 tablespoon butter and olive oil
- 1 pint (500 ml) vegetable stock
- ½ teaspoon sage and thyme
- ¼ teaspoon pepper

1 Heat the olive oil and butter in a saucepan and gently fry the onions, covered with a lid, until they are transparent.

2 Add the potato, parsnip and carrots, stir them around to coat them with oil. Cover and stew them until they are soft, about half an hour.

3 Add the stock, herbs and pepper and bring it to the boil. Simmer for 5 minutes then allow to cool slightly.

4 Whizz up in a blender until smooth, reheat and serve.

CARROTY WRAPS

- 4 soft flour tortilla wraps
- 1 tub of hummus
- 2 carrots, scrubbed and grated
- 1 cup of shredded lettuce
- Lemon juice
- Pepper

1 Lay the tortillas out flat and spread the center with a generous layer of hummus.

2 Divide the carrot evenly between the wraps and sprinkle it over the wrap, leaving a space all around the edge to make rolling up easier. Top the carrot with a sprinkle of crunchy lettuce.

3 Season the lettuce and carrot with a small squeeze of lemon juice and a grind of pepper.

4 Very carefully roll up the wrap and cut it in half.

ORANGEY CARROT BUTTERFLIES

For the cake:
- 4 oz (110 g) light brown sugar
- ⅓ pint (150 ml) sunflower oil
- 2 eggs, beaten
- 8 oz (200 g) self-raising flour
- 1 teaspoon cinnamon
- Zest of ½ a lemon and ½ an orange
- 5 oz (140 g) finely grated carrot

For the icing:
- 1 ½ oz (40 g) butter, softened
- 4 oz (110 g) icing sugar, sieved
- 1 tablespoon orange juice
- Zest of ½ and orange

1 Preheat the oven to 400° F (200° C). Place 12 muffin cases in a muffin tray.

2 Beat the sugar and the oil together and slowly add the eggs.

3 Gradually add the rest of the cake ingredients, stirring gently.

4 Spoon the batter into the muffin cases and bake in the oven for 20 minutes, or until a skewer inserted in the muffins comes out clean. Cool.

5 Prepare the icing by creaming all the ingredients together with a wooden spoon.

6 When the cakes are cool, slice off the tops and cut these in half. Spread a spoonful of icing on each cake and replace the tops at an angle, like butterfly wings.

BLUEBERRY POPSICLES

- 1 pint (500 ml) vanilla yogurt
- 1 tablespoon runny honey
- 2 cups blueberries

1 Combine all the ingredients together in a blender and whizz until smooth

2 Pour into popsicle moulds and freeze.

BLUEBERRY PANCAKES

- 8 oz (225 g) self-raising flour
- 1 tablespoon baking powder
- 2 large eggs
- 1 oz (30 g) butter, melted
- 11 fl oz (300 ml) milk
- 1 cup blueberries
- Sunflower oil

1 In a small bowl beat the eggs and add the milk and the melted butter.

2 Sift the flour and baking powder into a large bowl. Slowly add the liquid ingredients to the dry ingredients, beating well all the time.

3 When well mixed, set aside for 15 minutes. Meanwhile turn the oven on to a low heat, ready to keep the pancakes warm. Warm a heavy frying pan until it is medium-hot. Oil the bottom of the pan with one or two teaspoons of sunflower oil.

4 Stir the blueberries into the pancake batter and, when the pan is hot, add a tablespoon of the batter to the pan. Cook until the edges begin to dry out and bubbles appear in the middle of your pancake.

5 Flip the pancake over, cook the other side and transfer to the oven to keep warm. Continue until all the batter has been used up.

6 Serve with butter and warmed maple syrup

BLUEBERRY CREPES

- 4 oz (110 g) plain flour
- ½ pint (250 ml) milk
- 1 egg, beaten
- 2 cups blueberries, washed
- ½ pint whipped cream or thick yogurt and whipped cream, mixed
- Sugar or icing sugar for dusting
- Sunflower oil

1 Sift the flour into a mixing bowl and slowly add the milk, mixing well all the while. Add the beaten egg.

2 Heat a heavy frying pan and add a teaspoon of oil.

3 Using a ladle or a teacup, pour in enough batter to thinly coat the bottom of the pan.

4 When the underside is nicely brown, slide a spatula under the edge and gently flip your crepe over to cook on the other side. Set aside.

5 Continue to make your crepes in the same way until all the batter has been used up. Don't forget to add more oil to the pan when it is needed.

6 When all your crepes are made, you can begin to fill them. Divide the blueberries between the crepes and add a spoonful of cream or yogurt/cream mix. Fold or roll the crepes up to enclose the filling.

7 Just before serving, dust the top of each crepe with sugar or icing sugar.

PUMPKIN SOUP

- 2 tablespoons olive oil
- 2 onions, sliced
- 1 teaspoon sugar
- 5 lb (2 kg) pumpkin, peeled seeded and chopped
- 2 ½ pints (1.5 litres) vegetable stock
- ¼ teaspoon smoked paprika
- ¼ pint (125 ml) single cream
- 1 very pretty pumpkin, to serve
- 10 oz (250 g) croutons
- 10 oz (250 g) gruyère cheese, grated

1 In a large pan, cook the onions very gently in the oil and sugar.

2 When they are soft and golden brown, add the stock and the chopped pumpkin and the smoked paprika. Stir until combined, cover and leave to simmer over a medium heat for 15 to 20 minutes until the pumpkin is very soft. Using a blender, whizz the soup until smooth and then set aside until you are ready to serve.

3 Prepare your serving pumpkin by scooping out the flesh from the middle, making sure you remove all the seeds and stringy bits or loose bits that could find their way into the soup. Set aside until you are ready to serve.

4 When you are ready to serve, fill the pumpkin with very hot water and leave it to warm through.

5 Add the cream to the soup and reheat it gently. Empty the water out of the pumpkin, pat the inside dry and pour your soup into the pumpkin.

6 Serve with a bowl of croutons and lots of fresh bread.

ZUCCHINI DIPPERS

- 4 small to medium zucchinis
- 2 eggs, beaten
- 2 tablespoons flour
- 2 tablespoons milk
- 4 tablespoons dried breadcrumbs
- Salt, pepper and mixed dried herbs
- Oil for frying

1 Slice the zucchinis lengthwise to make batons about 4" (10 cm) long and ½" (1.5 cm) wide. Pat dry.

2 Arrange the eggs, flour, milk and breadcrumbs in individual bowls. Season the flour with plenty of pepper and mixed herbs. Add a pinch of salt.

3 Dip each zucchini baton into, first the egg, then flour, then milk and then breadcrumbs. Make sure all the zucchini is covered, and set aside on a plate.

4 Pour oil into a frying pan so that it is ½ inch deep and heat it until it is hot, but not smoking.

5 Carefully fry several batons at a time, turning them over until they are golden brown on all sides. Pat dry with absorbent kitchen paper.

6 When all the dippers are cooked serve up with a crispy salad, accompanied by tzatziki, ketchup or garlicky mayonnaise.

ZUCCHINI FUDGE CAKE

For the cake:
- 3 ½ oz (85 g) butter
- 1 cup granulated sugar
- 2 eggs
- 1 ¼ cups self-raising flour
- ⅓ cups cocoa powder
- ¼ cups milk (or less if batter is runny)
- 1 cup finely grated zucchini, including skin

For the icing:
- ⅔ cups icing sugar
- 2 ½ oz (70 g) butter, softened
- 2 tablespoons cocoa powder
- 2 teaspoons milk

1 Preheat the oven to 180° C (350° F). Grease and line the base of a 8 x 10" (10 x 20 cm) cake tin.

2 Place the grated zucchini in a colander to drip.

3 Cream the butter and sugar together until light and fluffy. Slowly beat in the eggs.

4 Sift the flour and cocoa into the egg mixture and stir in the zucchini.

5 Add the milk a little bit at a time until the batter is pourable but not runny.

6 Pour batter into the prepared tin and bake for about 45 minutes or until a knife inserted into the middle comes out clean.

7 Make the icing by dissolving cocoa in a tablespoon of boiling water, allow it to cool and the cream along with the remaining ingredients. Spread onto the cooled cake.

CUCUMBER PINWHEELS

- 8 large slices very soft white or brown bread, crusts removed
- Small tub cream cheese
- 1 tablespoon mayonnaise
- ½ a large cucumber, chopped small
- ½ a small sweet red pepper, chopped small

1 Mix together the cream cheese and the mayonnaise.

2 Spread one side of each slice of bread with the cheese mixture covering the whole surface.

3 Sprinkle the chopped cucumber and red pepper on top of the cream cheese, but leave a strip without any veggies at each of the short sides of the bread.

4 Roll the bread up, starting with a short side, until it is sausage shaped. Cut the roll into three or four pinwheels. Arrange on a plate.

ONE POT DILL PICKLES

- 2 cups thinly sliced cucumbers
- Iced water
- ½ teaspoon each dill seed and dill weed
- ¼ teaspoon pickling spice
- ½ cup cider vinegar
- ½ cup sugar
- ½ small onion, sliced

1 Soak the sliced cucumbers in the iced water in the fridge for two hours. Drain and pat dry.

2 Meanwhile combine all the other ingredients in a saucepan and bring to the boil. Simmer for 5 minutes. Then add cucumber and simmer for 3 minutes.

3 Pack the cucumbers into a large jar and fill to the brim with vinegar mix, making sure that all the seeds and spices are transferred to the jar. Seal the jar and store in the fridge.

4 These pickles can be eaten right away but the flavor will improve the longer you leave them.

TZATZIKI

- ½ pint (250 ml) of thick Greek yogurt
- ½ large cucumber, seeds removed
- Large handful mint leaves
- 1 garlic clove
- Squeeze of lemon juice
- Salt and pepper

1 Grate the cucumber and chop the mint finely.

2 Mince the garlic clove.

3 Combine all of the ingredients together and test for seasoning. You may want to add a touch more of one or more of the ingredients to taste.

4 This dip is best left for the flavors to develop for a day or so before eating, but it can be made and eaten right away if necessary.

5 Serve with zucchini dippers, falafel, chips or potatoes.

BLACKCURRANT TARTS

- 1 quantity shortcrust pastry, rolled thinly
- 1 cup blackcurrants, washed
- 1 scant tablespoon sugar
- 1 teaspoon flour
- Milk for glazing and sugar for dusting

1 Preheat the oven to 350° F (180° C) and prepare the tart tins by dusting liberally with flour.

2 In a small bowl, combine the blackcurrants, flour and sugar and set aside.

3 With a round cookie cutter, cut out 12 circles to fit your tart tins and place in the tins. Fill each one with teaspoon of blackcurrant mixture.

4 Cut out smaller circles for lids and place on the top of each tart. Brush each lid with milk and dust lightly with sugar.

5 Bake for 15 minutes until golden.

REDCURRANT CUPCAKES

For the cakes:
- 4 oz (110 g) soft butter or margarine
- 4 oz (110 g) sugar
- 2 eggs, beaten
- 4 oz (110 g) self-raising flour
- 1 tablespoon water

For the icing:
- 1 cup redcurrants, stripped and washed, plus a few to decorate
- 1 to 2 heaped tablespoons icing sugar

1 Preheat the oven to 400° F (200° C) and put paper cases in cupcake or small muffin tin.

2 Cream together the butter and sugar until light and fluffy.

3 Add the egg a bit at a time and beat after each addition.

4 Sieve in the flour and fold it into the mixture. Only add the water if the mixture is very stiff.

5 Bake in the oven for 15 minutes until the tops of the cakes are golden. Cool.

6 To make the icing, whizz the redcurrants in a blender with a little water until they are a smooth puree. Put the puree in a bowl and slowly add the sieved icing sugar a bit at a time until you have a very thick, spoonable mixture. Put a teaspoon of icing on each cake and top with a small sprig of redcurrants.

GOOSEBERRY FOOL

- ½ pint (250 ml) thick Greek yogurt
- ½ pint (250 ml) whipping cream, whipped
- 2 cups gooseberries, washed
- 2 tablespoons sugar

1 Place the gooseberries in a small saucepan, cover and cook on a gentle heat until the fruit is soft and juicy. Add the sugar and stir it until it has dissolved. Cool.

2 In a blender, whizz the gooseberries until they are smooth.

3 Gently mix the gooseberries, yogurt and cream together until well combined. Spoon into individual glasses and serve.

PASTA AND PEAS

- 1 bag fresh tagliatelle
- 1 tablespoon olive oil or butter
- 2 spring onions, finely chopped
- 1 cup peas
- 1 cup single cream
- Salt and pepper

1 Cook tagliatelle as directed on the packet. Drain, toss with a knob of butter and keep warm.

2 In a deep frying pan, fry the spring onions in oil or butter for 2 minutes, add the peas and cook for a further 3 minutes.

3 Add the cream and warm through without boiling.

4 Add the tagliatelle to the pan and toss in the creamy sauce until well coated.

5 Serve with a green salad and garlic bread.

CHEESY PEASY PUFFS

- ½ tablespoon chopped fresh mint leaves
- 2 oz (60 g) peas
- 4 oz (110 g) feta cheese, well rinsed and crumbled
- 1 pack ready- rolled puff pastry
- Pepper
- 1 egg, beaten

1 Preheat the oven to 350º F (180º C). Line a flat baking tray with baking paper.

2 Mix the mint, peas and feta cheese together and set aside.

3 Cut the pastry into eight equal rectangles and brush the edges of each rectangle with the beaten egg.

4 Divide the filling into eight and spoon in the center of each rectangle. Fold over to enclose the mixture inside, pressing the eggy edges together to seal.

5 Place the pastries on the baking sheet and bake in the oven for 25 minutes until lightly golden and well risen.

MILD CURRY PASTIES

- 1 cup cooked potato
- 1 cup fresh peas
- 1 tablespoon chopped onion
- 2 teaspoons oil
- 1 quantity shortcrust pastry
- 1 to 2 teaspoons mild curry paste
- Juice of ½ a lemon
- Small handful coriander
- Milk for glazing

1 Preheat the oven to 350º F (180º C). Line a baking tray with baking paper.

2 Roll the pastry out onto a floured surface and, using a bowl, cut rounds of pastry and set them out on the baking tray. Brush the edges with milk to help seal the edges when they are folded.

3 Heat the oil in a frying pan and fry the onion on low heat until transparent. Add the peas and cook for 2 minutes and add the potato, lemon juice and the curry paste. Stir around and, if too dry, add a tablespoon of water. When the consistency is just right, remove from the heat and stir in the chopped coriander.

4 Spoon the mixture onto the center of each pastry round and fold to make a semi-circle. Pinch the edges to seal and brush the pastry with milk to glaze.

5 Cook in the oven for 20 minutes until golden brown. Serve with chutney or yogurt.

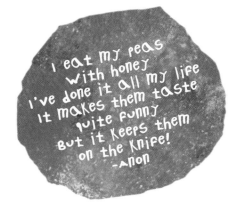

I eat my peas with honey
I've done it all my life
It makes them taste quite funny
But it keeps them on the knife!
-Anon

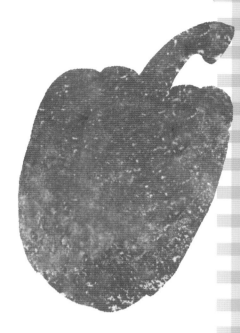

PEPPER POTS

- 4 cups cooked rice
- 5 red peppers
- ½ yellow pepper
- ½ cup peas
- 2 large spring (salad) onions, chopped
- 1 egg, beaten
- 1 stock cube dissolved in ¼ cup boiling water
- Handful of fresh mixed herbs such as basil, mint, thyme and marjoram, chopped.
- 2 tablespoons olive and sunflower oil, mixed

1 Preheat the oven to 350° F (180° C). Oil a shallow oven proof dish and set aside.

2 Cut the top off four of the red peppers and scoop out the seeds and all of the bitter white pith. Season the inside of the peppers with salt and pepper. Keep the tops to use as lids for your pepper pots.

3 Chop the ½ yellow pepper and the remaining whole red pepper.

4 Heat the oil in a wok or deep frying pan. Add the onions and fry for 2 minutes. Add the chopped peppers and fry for a further 4 minutes. Add the peas, rice and the stock/water mixture and stir until well combined.

5 When the rice has warmed through, make a space in the center of the pan and pour in the egg. Leave it until it begins to set, give it a stir and leave it to set again.

6 Spoon the rice into the pepper pots and top with their lids. Reserve the extra rice and keep warm. Place the peppers in the oven for about 20 to 30 minutes until the pepper pots are just beginning to become tender, then serve, accompanied by the extra reserved rice.

PEPPER AND HALLOUMI SKEWERS

- 1 each large red yellow and orange pepper, seeded and cut into 1 inch chunks
- 1 large block of halloumi cheese, drained and cut into ½ inch cubes
- 2 tablespoons olive oil
- 1 large handful of mixed herbs, such as basil, marjoram, thyme and rosemary
- Black pepper

1 In a medium sized bowl combine all the ingredients and leave to marinate for at least half an hour.

2 Thread the peppers and halloumi onto wooden or metal skewers and grill or barbeque until the halloumi begins to brown.

3 Serve with a fresh couscous and a green salad.

POTATO WEDGES

- 4 large baking potatoes
- 2 tablespoons sunflower oil
- 3 teaspoon Cajun seasoning

1 Preheat the oven to 430° F (220° C).

2 Cut the potatoes in half lengthwise, then cut each half into four or five long wedges.

3 Place the wedges in a mixing bowl and sprinkle with the oil and toss until well covered.

4 Sprinkle the Cajun seasoning over the potatoes and stir until evenly coated.

5 Lay the wedges on a non-stick baking tray and place in the oven to cook for 15 minutes. Remove from the oven, carefully turn the wedges over so they brown evenly, and replace in the oven for another 15 to 20 minutes.

6 Serve with ketchup or mayonnaise.

ROSTI

- 1 lb (450 g) potatoes
- 1 handful chopped chives
- Salt and pepper
- 4 tablespoons sunflower oil

1 Peel and quarter the potatoes and place them in a saucepan. Cover with water, bring them to the boil and simmer for 5 minutes. Drain.

2 When cool, grate them with a coarse grater. Gently mix in the chopped chives and season the mix with salt and pepper.

3 Heat the oil in a frying pan over a medium heat. Add the potato mixture and press it down to make one large cake, or shape it into several smaller shapes and fry them in batches.

4 Cook the rosti until it is golden brown on one side, then turn it gently to finish browning on the reverse.

5 Serve with sliced cucumbers and peppers and tomatoes, with ketchup or the Tzatziki on page 82.

FRITTATA

- 4 eggs
- 1 tablespoon chopped chives or spring onions
- 1 clove garlic, very finely chopped
- 1 cup cooked peas
- 2 cups sliced waxy potatoes
- Salt and pepper
- 2 tablespoons sunflower oil

1 Heat the oil in a frying pan and add the onions or chives, and the potatoes. Fry these until they are heated through and they begin to brown. Turn them over and fry until they begin to brown on the other side.

2 Add the garlic and cook for one minute, then add the peas and heat until warmed through.

3 Beat the eggs, season and add to the pan. Stir once to coat the potatoes, then cover and leave the mixture to set.

4 Heat the grill. Once the bottom of the frittata is set, place the pan under the grill to finish off. Serve with fresh bread and a salad.

RASPBERRY FIZZ

- 1 lb (450 g) raspberries
- 1 lb (450 g) sugar

1 In a medium saucepan simmer the raspberries for about 20 minutes.

2 Strain the fruit and juice through a fine sieve three times, discarding the seeds and pulp.

3 Return the clear juice to the pan and add the sugar. Stir until the sugar is dissolved and simmer for 10 minutes. Leave to cool.

4 Prepare a screw topped bottle or jar by washing and drying it very thoroughly. Pour the syrup into the bottle using a funnel.

5 Dilute to taste with fizzy water and serve.

ONE POT RASPBERRY JAM

- 1 lb (450 g) raspberries
- 1 lb (450 g) sugar

1 Thoroughly wash and dry a large jar and its lid. With the lid on, stand the jar on a wooden surface and leave aside. Put a small plate in the freezer and leave to get cold.

2 In a saucepan, simmer the raspberries gently for 20 minutes. Add the sugar, stir until dissolved, then boil for about 30 minutes.

3 Take the plate from the freezer and put a teaspoon of jam on the plate and return it to the freezer. After a minute test to see if your jam has set by pushing the jam with a finger; if the jam wrinkles it is ready. If it is still liquid it need to be boiled for a few minutes longer and tested for a set again.

4 When the jam has set, cover and leave it to cool for 20 to 30 minutes.

5 Using a funnel or a ladle, fill the jar and seal with the lid. Store in the fridge.

SUMMER PUDDING

- 1 lb (450 g) raspberries
- 1 lb (450 g) mixed currants, gooseberries, and strawberries.
- 3 oz (85 g) sugar
- 10 slices day old bread, crusts removed

1 Place all the fruit in a saucepan and simmer for 5 minutes. Add the sugar and stir until dissolved. Set aside.

1 Line the base and sides of a pudding basin with the bread, patching until there are no gaps.

1 Ladle the juice and fruit into the basin. It may be necessary to encourage the juice to soak into the bread by gently easing the bread away from the edges in places and pouring some of the juice down the gap. Carefully pat everything in place, and finish with a well-fitting lid of bread.

1 Place a saucer over the bread lid, place a weight on top and leave overnight.

1 To serve, slide a knife down between the basin and the bread to release the pudding. Put a large plate on top of the basin and upturn the pudding onto the plate. Serve with cream.

RHUBARB CRUMBLE

- ⅓ cup butter
- 1 ⅓ cup brown sugar
- ¼ cup plain flour
- ⅔ cup rolled oats
- 4 cups chopped rhubarb

1 Preheat oven to 350° F (180° C).

2 Rub together butter and brown sugar until it resembles breadcrumbs. Rub in the flour and oats and cinnamon.

3 Put the chopped rhubarb into a baking dish, stir in sugar and sprinkle whit the crumb mixture.

4 Bake in the oven for 30 minutes or until the crumbs are golden brown.

5 Serve warm with ice-cream, cream or Greek yogurt.

RHUBARB SUNDAE

- 3 cups chopped rhubarb
- 1 tablespoon water
- 1 tablespoon brown sugar
- 1 pint (500 ml) vanilla yogurt
- 8 chocolate ginger biscuits
- Chocolate shavings

1 Stew the rhubarb by placing the water and rhubarb in a saucepan over a medium heat until it has reduced to a thick pulp. Add the sugar, stir until dissolved and leave to cool completely.

2 Crush the ginger biscuits and divide the crumbs between four glasses.

3 Spoon alternate layers of rhubarb and yogurt on top of the ginger crumbs, finishing with a layer of yogurt.

4 Top the sundaes off with a generous dusting of chocolate shavings.

RHUBARB FLAPJACKS
WITH CHOCOLATE DRIZZLE

- 1 lb (450 g) jumbo rolled oats
- 12 oz (350 g) butter or margarine
- 12 oz (350 g) dark brown sugar
- 4 tablespoons golden syrup
- 3 cups chopped rhubarb
- 1 tablespoon water
- ½ large bar of chocolate
- 1 tablespoon milk
- 1 small beetroot, peeled and quartered, if available to color your rhubarb

1 Preheat the oven to 325° F (160° C). Oil an 8 x 10 x 1½" cake tin (20 x 25 x 6 cm), line it with baking paper and oil it again.

2 Put the chopped rhubarb and the water in a saucepan on a medium heat. Cover and leave to stew until it is reduced to a thick pulp.

3 In another saucepan melt the butter, sugar and golden syrup together until the sugar has dissolved. Remove from the heat and add the oats.

4 Spoon ½ the oat mixture into the prepared tin and spread it around with the back of a metal spoon. Spoon the stewed rhubarb evenly over the oats and finish off with a layer of the remaining oat mixture.

5 Bake in the oven for 30 minutes until the flapjacks are bubbling and golden brown. Remove from the oven and leave to cool for ½ an hour. Turn out onto a plate and cut into squares using an oiled knife.

6 Melt the chocolate and milk together and drizzle over the flapjacks. Leave to cool and set.

SUPER SALAD SCOOBIE SNACK

- 12 slices fresh bread
- 2 large tomatoes, cut into slices
- 1 medium cucumber, cut into thin slices
- 1 small carrot, grated
- 1 handful chives, finely chopped
- 1 handful Greek basil, finely chopped
- Few sprigs of marjoram, finely chopped
- 8 slices medium cheddar or other good flavored cheese
- 2 tablespoons mayonnaise
- Salt and pepper

1 Lay four slices of bread out onto four plates. Spread mayonnaise on top of each slice. Arrange some salad leaves on top, followed by one slice of cheese, followed by the sliced tomato. Sprinkle some of the mixed herbs over the tomato and add a grind of pepper.

2 Cover this with the next slice of bread and spread with another teaspoon of mayonnaise. Sprinkle on some grated carrot, top with another slice of cheese and finish with the sliced cucumber, sprinkled with herbs, salt and pepper.

3 Cover with the last slice of bread and press the stack down gently. Carefully cut the sandwich in half and stack one half on top of the other. Insert a skewer through the stack to keep them in place and serve with a few crisps and slices of apple.

SALMON CAESAR SALAD

- Salad leaves
- 4 thick slices day old bread, crusts removed
- 1 garlic clove
- 1 tablespoon olive oil
- 4 small responsible-farmed salmon fillets
- 4 tablespoons Caesar salad dressing

1 Preheat the oven to 350° F (180° C).

2 Cut the garlic in half lengthwise and rub the cut sides all over the both sides of the bread. With a pastry brush, paint both sides of the bread lightly with olive oil. Cut the bread into cubes, place on a baking tray and toast in the oven until golden and crisp. Set aside.

3 Tear the salad leaves into bite sized pieces and drizzle with salad dressing and toss to coat. Divide the leaves between four shallow bowls.

4 Press the salmon fillets until they are of an even thickness. Season with salt and pepper. Sear the fillets in a hot frying pan until crisp and golden, then turn and cook on the other side.

5 Scatter the croutons evenly over the salad leaves, break the salmon fillets into large chunks and lay the salmon on top of the leaves. Serve while still hot with crusty bread.

FLOWER POWER SALAD

- 1 head lettuce or other salad leaves, washed
- A handful of any of the following: shredded mint or basil leaves, chopped dill, thyme, marjoram, parsley or snipped chives
- A good handful of petals of any of the following flowers: nasturtiums, chives, borage, violets, rosemary, sage, calendula, roses, thyme or lavender.

1 Shred the lettuce by hand into a serving bowl.

2 Mix in the chopped or shredded herbs.

3 Scatter the flower petals on the top and arrange prettily.

4 Serve with a light salad dressing on the side.

STRAWBERRY SHAKE

- 20 strawberries
- 2 cups milk
- 2 cups vanilla ice-cream
- A little honey to sweeten

1 Put all the ingredients into a blender... put the lid on!

2 Whizz everything up and pour it into glasses.

STRAWBERRY SHORTCAKE

- 2 cups plain flour
- ⅓ cup sugar, plus 1 tablespoon
- 3 teaspoons baking powder
- ½ cup butter or margarine
- 1 cup milk
- 3 cups strawberries, quartered

1 Preheat the oven to 425° F (220° C). Prepare a shallow baking tray by dusting it with flour.

2 Place quartered strawberries, washed and still wet, into a small saucepan.

3 Cover and heat gently until the juices begin to run. Add 1 tablespoon of sugar and stir until dissolved. Set aside.

4 For the scones, sift all the dry ingredients into a bowl.

5 Add the butter and, with a knife, cut the butter into the flour. Rub the flour and butter between your fingers until it begins to look like breadcrumbs.

6 Add the milk and stir the mixture with a fork until it sticks together like a soft dough. Change to using your hands and knead it and roll it until it is well mixed and smooth.

7 On a floured surface, press the dough out to about ¾" (2 cm) thick, then cut into 1" (2.5 cm) rounds with a cookie cutter.

8 Place on the floured baking tray and cook in the oven for about 15 minutes.

9 Serve, split open, with the strawberries and ice-cream.

STRAWBERRY TRIFLES

- 4 trifle sponges or portions of sponge cake
- 1 packet strawberry flavor vegetarian jelly
- 1 cup strawberries, quartered
- 1 ½ cups Greek yogurt, sweetened with honey

1 Break up the sponge and place in the bottoms of four glasses or small bowls.

2 Divide the strawberries between the glasses.

3 Make up the jelly according to the instructions on the packet and pour over the strawberries and sponge, leaving a space of about 1 inch at the top of the glass.

4 Place in the fridge to set. When set, spoon the yogurt on top of the jelly and serve.

BBQ CORN

- 8 Corn on the cob
- Salt and pepper
- 8 teaspoons butter

1 Take the husks and the silks off the corn cobs. Be sure to remove every bit of silk, so that you can really enjoy your corn.

2 Carefully lower the corn into a pan of boiling water, let it return to the boil and simmer for 5 minutes. Remove from the water and allow to cool.

3 Lay each cob on a large rectangle of silver foil. Add a teaspoon of butter, a grind of pepper and shake of salt to each one and wrap tightly, making sure there are no gaps for the butter or juices to escape.

4 Set these aside until the BBQ is ready, then place on the grill, and cook over the coals or 1 or 2 minutes each side.

CORN FRITTERS

- 5 oz (140 g) self-raising flour
- 1 egg, beaten
- 3½ fl oz (100 ml) milk
- 1 cup corn kernels
- 1 tablespoon sunflower oil
- Greek yogurt
- chilli jam or sweet chilli dipping sauce

1 Sift the flour into a medium sized bowl and slowly whisk in the milk and egg. Stir in the corn and season with salt and pepper.

2 Heat the oil in a frying pan over a medium/hot heat. Fry the fritters a tablespoon at a time in the oil until golden brown on both sides and drain on kitchen paper. Keep hot.

3 When all the fritters are cooked, serve them with thick Greek yogurt and chilli sauce.

CORN RELISH AND TOASTED HALLOUMI

- 1 pack halloumi cheese
- 1 large corn on the cob
- 1 small tin pineapple in juice
- 2 teaspoons finely chopped mild onion
- 2 tablespoons olive oil
- ½ tablespoon lemon juice
- pinch of chilli flakes

1 Boil the corn on the cob for 3 minutes and allow to cool.

2 Hold the corn firmly by one end while the other end rests on a chopping board and carefully cut downwards to cut the kernels off the cob.

3 Put the kernels in a dry frying pan and heat them, stirring occasionally, until a few of them are lightly browned. Set aside.

4 Drain the pineapple and reserve 1 tablespoon of juice. Chop the pineapple and place in a medium bowl along with the reserved juice, corn, onion, oil, lemon juice, chilli flakes. Set aside for the flavors to develop.

5 Rinse and dry the halloumi and cut it into ½" (1.5 cm) slices. Brush with oil and place on a baking sheet and grill under a high heat until they begin to brown. Turn them over, brush the other sides with oil and brown. Serve with the salsa and a some crusty bread.

CHEESE AND TOMATO TART

- 1 sheet ready-rolled puff pastry
- 2 cups cherry tomatoes, halved
- 8 oz (225 g) gruyère cheese
- Milk
- Small handful shredded Greek basil

1 Put the tomatoes in a small bowl and add salt and pepper. Stir and set aside.

2 Preheat the oven to 350º F (180º C). Prepare a baking sheet by lining it with baking paper.

3 Fold the edges of the puff pastry to make a rim around the edge and brush the rim with milk.

4 Scatter the tomatoes, cheese and basil evenly over the pastry and bake for 15 to 20 minutes until the pastry is risen and golden brown.

5 Serve with a green salad.

PIZZA/ PASTA SAUCE

- 10 medium tomatoes
- 2 cloves garlic, minced
- 2 onions, chopped
- 1 green pepper, finely chopped
- 1 teaspoon sugar
- 1 tablespoon chopped marjoram
- 1 tablespoon chopped basil

1 Cut a cross in the skin at the base of each tomato and place all of the tomatoes in a large bowl and cover them with boiling water. Leave them in the water for 2 minutes, then carefully lift them out, wait for them to cool for a minute and peel the skins away.

2 In a deep frying pan, fry the onions and garlic until transparent. Add the green pepper and fry for a further 2 minutes. Add the chopped tomatoes, cover and simmer gently for 30 minutes.

3 Add the sugar and the herbs, cook for 1 minute and allow to cool.

4 Transfer to a blender and whizz until smooth.

5 Use right away as pizza topping or pasta sauce or store in the freezer.

TOMATO AND FETA SALAD

- 1 standard pack feta cheese, cubed
- 2 cups tomatoes, cut into small chunks
- 1 clove garlic, minced
- 1 large handful basil, shredded
- 1 small handful mint and marjoram, finely chopped
- pepper

1 Combine all the ingredients in a bowl, place in the fridge for the flavors to develop.

2 Serve with crusty bread, spooned into pitta pockets or mixed with cold pasta.

ALPHABET SOUP

- 2 pints (1 litre) vegetable stock cubes
- 2 carrots
- 1 stick celery
- ½ small swede
- 1 cup of dried alphabet pasta shapes
- 1 large bunch of mixed herbs such as rosemary, marjoram, sage, chives and thyme

1 Chop all the vegetables into small chunks and add to the water and the powdered stock cubes in a saucepan. Bring to the boil and simmer gently until the vegetables are soft.

2 Either scoop out the softened vegetables and reserve them to use in another dish or leave them in for added flavor. Add the finely chopped herbs and the alphabet shapes to the saucepan and bring back to the boil. Cook for the time specified on the pasta packet.

3 Serve immediately.

MINTY ICE-CREAM

- ½ pint (300 ml) double or whipping cream
- ½ pint (300 ml) natural yogurt
- 2 tablespoons milk
- 5 tablespoons icing sugar, sieved
- 1 large handful of mint leaves, very finely chopped
- 1 large handful of chocolate chips

1 Place a container in the freezer to chill. An old ice-cream tub is ideal.

2 Pour the cream, yogurt and milk into a mixing bowl and beat them with a whisk or an electric mixer until thick.

3 Add the icing sugar and the mint and stir until well combined. Stir in the chocolate chips.

4 Pour the mixture into the chilled container and return it to the freezer for 1 or 2 hours. Using a fork, break up the ice crystals which have formed and mix it until it is smooth. Return the container to the freezer for another hour and then mix it once more to break up the ice crystals. Return it to the freezer for a final time and leave it to set.

5 Remove the container from the freezer and place it in the fridge for half an hour before serving.

HERBY SCONES

- 5 oz (140 g) self-raising flour
- 1 teaspoon baking powder
- 1 oz (30 g) cold butter or margarine
- 4 fl. oz (125 ml) milk
- 2 ½ oz (70 g) grated cheese
- 2 to 3 tablespoons finely chopped mixed herbs such as chives, rosemary and marjoram

1 Preheat the oven to 400° F (200° C) and grease and flour a shallow baking tray.

2 Put all the dry ingredients, including the cheese, into a bowl. Add the butter and rub it into the dry ingredients using your fingers. Keep on rubbing it until the mixture looks like breadcrumbs.

3 Add the milk, stirring it in with a fork until blended and then finish mixing it with your hands until it has become a soft, but not sticky, dough.

4 Press the dough out onto a well floured surface until it is about 1" (2.5 cm) thick.

5 With a cookie cutter, cut the dough into 2" (5 cm) rounds and place them onto the baking tray. Brush the tops of each round with a little milk.

6 Cook in the oven for 15 to 20 minutes until well risen and golden brown.

GLOSSARY

Anthers the male part of the flower which holds the pollen.

Anti-clockwise the opposite to the direction that a clock's hands move around the clock face.

Bush a type of plant that has many branches rather than one main stem.

Calcium a mineral needed for healthy growth.

Carbon dioxide gas that plants use in photosynthesis but that is damaging to the environment in high quantities.

Cells the building blocks that all living things are made of.

Chemical a substance that can be good or bad and can be mixed together to make other substances.

Chit to encourage potatoes to grow shoots before they are planted.

Chlorophyll the green substance in plants that stores the sun's energy.

Clay a type of earth that is made of very tiny particles.

Climate the regular weather conditions of an area.

Clockwise the direction a clock's hands moves around the clock face.

Companion plants plants that help other plants.

Compost soil made from the decayed remains of kitchen and garden waste.

Cordon a way of growing plants on a single stem.

Cross-pollination when different varieties of plants pollinate each other.

Eco-friendly products or methods of doing things that will not harm the world.

Ericaceous a type of soil that is needed by blueberries and other acid-loving plants.

Ethylene gas a gas that helps fruit to ripen. Ethylene gas is released by bananas as they ripen.

Evaporation the process where water changes from a liquid to a gas (water vapor).

Eyes (potato) the parts of the potato that will grow into the shoots and stems.

Gas a substance that is not liquid or solid at room temperature.

Germination the time when a seed splits open and turns into a plant.

Grafted the stem of one plant is attached to the root of another to make it grow in a certain way.

Hardy a plant that will tolerate cold conditions.

Heavy soil a soil that is difficult to dig because it contains lots of clay and so traps a lot of water.

Hemisphere half a sphere, the half of the world above (Northern) or below (Southern) the equator.

Hibernate to go into a sleepy state in the colder months of the year so not to have to find food.

Honeydew a sweet, sticky liquid made by aphids and other insects.

Humus natures compost. A type of soil made naturally from rotten remains of plants and animals.

Invasive a plant that will produce so many roots or new plants that it becomes a pest.

Lime a chemical essential to plant growth that also makes the soil alkaline.

Mammal warm-blooded animal that gives birth to live young and feeds them with milk.

Micro-organisms tiny creatures that need a magnifying glass or micro-scope to be seen.

Mild not too hot or too cold.

Moisture water.

Mulch a layer of material, natural or man made, that covers an area of soil.

Nectar a sugary liquid made by flowers to attract pollinators.

Night soil people poo!

Nitrogen and element found in the air and the soil that is necessary for plant growth.

Nutrients plant foods, available naturally in the soil or in home-made or bought fertilizers.

Organic in gardening it is used to mean anything that doesn't contain harmful (especially man-made) chemicals.

Oxygen a gas that is essential to life.

Peat a type of soil made from decayed plants. Peat takes thousands of years to make.

Peat-free any type of soil which does not contain any peat. The only type to buy.

Phosphate an element that is essential for plant growth.

Potash another name for potassium

Potassium an element essential to healthy plant growth.

Reptiles cold blooded creatures, usually with scaly skin.

Rooting powder a chemical, either man-made or natural that will encourage roots to grow from a cut stem or leaf.

Runners a long flexible stem designed to grow away from the mother plant and send down new roots.

Sand a course type of soil made from ground up rocks.

Seaweed gel a jelly-like substance made from seaweed that swells up to hold on to water that would otherwise drain away.

Shoots the growing tips of stems or branches.

Silks the hairy part of the corn cob that pokes out of the top of the enclosing leaves. The silks are actually the styles, the female tubes that lead down to the kernels, which are the ovules.

Slow-release fertilizer a plant food that is made to let its goodness be released over several weeks rather than all at once.

Tender a plant that dies if it gets too cold.

Thinnings seedlings or plantlets that are pulled up to give the remaining plants space to grow.

Tonic a liquid plant food applied to give a plant a boost.

Trench a long narrow hole.

Variegated leaves which are marked with yellow or white (sometimes other colors) as well as green.

Water saving crystals a man-made substance that swells up and holds water rather than letting water drain away.

QUIZ ANSWERS

Page 6

Roots that you can eat… carrots, potatoes (actually the bit we eat is classed as a stem by scientists!), turnips, yams, sweet potatoes, swede, parsnip, beetroot, radishes, garlic….

Stems that you can eat… asparagus, rhubarb, celery, kohlrabi , leeks, onions, broccoli, cauliflower….

Leaves that you can eat… lettuce, cabbage, kale, beets, purslane, parsley, dandelions, brussel sprouts, basil, beets….

Flowers that you can eat… broccoli, cauliflower, zucchini, artichokes, elderflowers, roses, nasturtiums, chives, violets, sunflowers, pot marigolds, pansies….

Seeds that you can eat… sunflower, sesame, beans, peas, pumpkin, corn, rice, wheat, peanuts, nuts….

Page 10

Sweet fruit and tasty seeds tempt animals and birds to eat them. As the animals travel around they drop some of the fruit and eat and excrete (poo) some seeds.

Fluffy and light-weight seeds are caught by the wind and blown far away from the parent plant.

Spiny and sticky seeds attach onto the fur of passing animals. When the animal grooms itself the seed is released and falls to the ground.

Exploding capsules can be triggered to release their seeds by touch or movement, and can shoot the seeds several feet away from the parent plant.

The oldest living seed is a 2,000 year old Judean Date Palm which was found in a pottery jar in Herod the Greats' tomb in Israel. It is now growing into a tree.

Page 23

Amphibians you could find in your garden could include frogs, toads and newts.

Small mammals you could find in your garden could include mice, moles, hedgehogs, shrews, squirrels badgers and foxes… with bats over your garden.

Reptiles you could find in your garden could include lizards, snakes and slow worms… in warmer climates you may find tortoises and turtles too.

Page 38

Runner beans are the only edible plant that twines anti-clockwise in the Northern Hemisphere and clockwise in the Southern Hemisphere.

Page 44

The carrots eaten by Europeans in the olden days were purple, red, white or yellow, never orange.

Page 45

In the rationing and black-outs of World War Two Britain, carrots were one of the few vegetables in plentiful supply. The government came up with the idea of telling children that carrots could help them to see in the dark to help spot enemy planes… it worked and carrot consumption rose enormously.

Page 46

One blueberry can produce more than 6,000 berries in one year.

Page 50

Cucumbers are 98% water!

Most plants tendrils twist clockwise in the northern hemisphere and anti-clockwise in the southern hemisphere.

Page 56

The real answer is "It depends on how big his pickled peppers were." To make it easier to figure out it helps to know that a peck is the same as 16 pints. So if one pint could hold about ten medium sized pickled peppers, how many could 16 pints hold? 160 of course. However, the real question is, how did Peter Piper find a pepper bush that grew peppers that were already pickled?

Page 67

None. But there are an average of 200 seeds on the outside of a strawberry… go on, count them!

Page 69

The tallest sunflower to date was a whopping 25½ feet tall!

Page 73

When tomatoes were first taken from the Andes to Spain 500 years ago they were called pomo d'oro… golden apple. This tells us that tomatoes were yellow, not red as they usually are today.

DEDICATION AND THANKS!

This book is dedicated to my family; to my Mum, Mark and Toby for their constant faith and to my super girls, Bex and Issy for being my champions and willing companions throughout the adventures of the book.

I'd like to say a huge thank you to all the children who helped me with the photographs for this book… to those who ignored the camera and diligently carried on gardening and to those who hammed it up marvellously. I enjoyed working with all of you. To Lizzie and the gang; Will, Eddie and George and to Lois, the natural model. Thanks to Molly and Eve and to Luke and Emma. Thanks also to the Chalford Hill Gardening Club members; Eliza, Millie, Emily, Isabella, Lottie and Marcus. Huge thanks to Wendy and Lucy for your recipes and to Alice, the keenest gardener, for your bubbling enthusiasm. My biggest thanks goes, of course, to my Issy, because you were always ready whenever the sun peeped out and to Bex, because without you the photographs would still be locked up in the camera instead of illustrating the pages of this book!

Elizabeth McCorquodale

Black Dog Publishing Limited
10a Acton Street
London WC1X 9NG
United Kingdom
info@blackdogonline.com

Edited and designed by Black Dog Publishing, London, UK. Illustrations by Stella Macdonald.

ISBN 978 1 906155 92 6

British Library Cataloguing-in-Publication Data. A CIP record for this book is available from the British Library.

Black Dog Publishing Limited, London, UK, is an environmentally responsible company. *Kids in the Garden* is printed on an FSC certified paper.

architecture art design
fashion history photography
theory and things

www.blackdogonline.com